HAGGAI, ZECHARIAH, & MALACHI

A SELF-STUDY GUIDE

Irving L. Jensen

MOODY PRESS

CHICAGO

Contents

Introduction 4

1. Historical Setting of the Postexilic Prophets 7

HAGGAI
2. Background and Survey of Haggai 17
3. "Build the House" 25
4. "I Will Fill This House with Glory" 32

ZECHARIAH
5. Background and Survey of Zechariah 42
6. Zechariah's Night Visions 48
7. What About Fasting? 60
8. Israel's History to the End of Time 65
9. King over All 71

MALACHI
10. Background and Survey of Malachi 76
11. "Will a Man Rob God?" 81
    Bibliography 88

Introduction

The closing years of the Old Testament were crucial ones in world history. Powerful leaders were emerging in nations around the world, attracting the masses to their own man-made religions and philosophies. Among such men were Confucius, in China, 551-479 B.C.; Buddha, in India, 563-483 B.C.; Zoroaster, in Iran, sixth century B.C.; Thales, in Greece, 640-546 B.C. Haggai and Zechariah, two of the Lord's prophets studied in this manual, were contemporaries of some of those leaders.

It should interest us to know what God was saying to His chosen people in Canaan during the last era of the Old Testament. And when we learn from His prophets, we have the assurance that they spoke the truth of God, not the fallible reasonings of a Confucius or Buddha. This is but one of the many incentives to study the books of this self-study guide: *Haggai, Zechariah, and Malachi.*

Some Practical Hints for Personal Bible Study

There is no mystical, mechanical formula for effective Bible study. But the conscientious Christian, sensitive to the Spirit's teaching, can become a better Bible student—and a stronger Christian—by consistently following proved study principles. Here are some suggestions:

1. Study the Bible for yourself. This does not mean you should reject help from others (e.g., from commentaries). But it will surprise you how much you yourself can see in the Bible text, with the enlightening ministry of the Holy Spirit, before turning to outside help.

2. Respect the Bible for what it is and what it can do for you. You must be convinced that it is truly God's Word, authoritative and dependable. And you must have the will to learn from it what

4

God wants you to learn. Your determination to study will be your most effective weapon against the ever-present enemy "No Time."

3. Study in an orderly, organized way. Method is simply orderly procedure. Flitting here and there, without purpose, is frustrating and will accomplish little.

4. Study out of one basic translation. Highly recommended translations are the King James Version and the *New American Standard Bible*. Modern language translations and paraphrases (e.g., *The Living Bible*) may be referred to in the course of your study of a basic version, to clarify obscure phrases. The important rule here is: Analyze the basic translation; compare modern paraphrases.

5. Study the Bible the way God wrote it: book by book. This is the approach of these study guides.

6. Get an overall view, then look at the content in more detail. In studying a particular book, consider first its background (e.g., its authorship); then survey its overall structure; then analyze each chapter in detail. Most of your study should be in the analysis phase.

7. Try the inductive approach. This is basically a simple and natural way to study. As applied to Bible study, it includes (1) directly examining the Bible text; (2) letting it speak for itself; and (3) basing conclusions only on observations. Observation is a key ingredient of inductive study. The order of all Bible study should be (1) observation (what does it say?); (2) interpretation (what does it mean?); (3) application (how does this apply to me and to others?). It is amazing how much the Bible interprets itself when you have first thoroughly observed what it says.

8. Distinguish between content and form. When you observe such things as historical facts and doctrines in a Bible passage, you are observing content. When you note how that content is organized in the author's writing, you are studying its form (structure). The difference between studying isolated words and words in context is like the difference between seeing piles of building materials on a lot and seeing a constructed house on an adjacent lot. In this connection it is interesting to note how God did *not* choose to write His revelation. For example, the Bible is not an encyclopedia, organized alphabetically; nor is it a book of doctrines organized topically. Most of it is history and biography, involving people like yourself. God chose to communicate His revelation in the setting of humanity. Divine doctrines are taught, for example, as they relate to man.

9. Write out your observations as you study the Bible text. "The pencil is one of the best eyes." This study manual will offer many suggestions for recording your observations.

5

10. Keep God's purposes clearly in mind. Your goals in studying the Bible should coincide with God's purposes in giving it: "All scripture is given by inspiration of God, and is profitable for doctrine, for reproof, for correction, for instruction in righteousness: that the man of God may be perfect, thoroughly furnished unto all good works" (2 Tim. 3:16-17). When Peter wrote, "Grow in grace, and in the knowledge of our Lord and Saviour Jesus Christ" (2 Pet. 3:18), he had in mind the Scriptures as the source of that growth and knowledge (2 Pet. 3:16). The success of any method of Bible study is measured here.

Postscript

This particular manual is my concluding work in the self-study series covering all the books of the Bible. It is difficult for me to express how satisfying and enjoyable this experience has been. I have learned more of what God has written in His book, and that to me is priceless. It has been my continuing prayer that God would use the study guides to help others see and appropriate the matchless treasures of His Word. The Bible is the only Book God has written for us, and that is reason enough to acclaim it as the greatest of all books.

I want to express thanks to Moody Press for the invitation to write these books, and for the help and encouragement that the staff has given to me through many years of the project. And the constant support and labors of my wife, Charlotte, including typing the manuscripts, were a major key to the uninterrupted progress of the series. I am deeply grateful to God for such inspiring fellowship in the ministry of His Word.

Lesson 1

Historical Setting of the Postexilic Prophets

Haggai, Zechariah, and Malachi were Israel's last writing prophets in Old Testament Times. They were called postexilic prophets because they served after the Jews had returned to Canaan from exile in Babylon. See Chart A. Who were the preexilic prophets, and who were the exilic prophets? Do you see why the postexilic prophets are also called the restoration prophets?

It can be seen from this chart that a natural order of studying the Bible's prophetic books would be (1) preexilic, (2) exilic, and (3) postexilic.

This lesson is devoted to a study of the historical setting of Haggai, Zechariah, and Malachi. The Bible text of the three books comes alive to you if, among other things, you have seen what situations moved God to commission the three prophets to write.[1]

I. POSTEXILIC PROPHETS IN THE OLD TESTAMENT CANON

Refer to the list (canon) of Old Testament books in the opening pages of your Bible. Where do the names Haggai, Zechariah, and Malachi appear? What books in the list do you associate with the following groups:

> five books of the law
> twelve books of history
> five books of poetry
> five books of major prophets (beginning with Isaiah)
> twelve books of minor prophets[2] (beginning with Hosea)

---

1. The prophets also preached many, if not all, of the messages they were divinely inspired to write.
2. The designations *major* and *minor* represent the length of each book, not the relative importance.

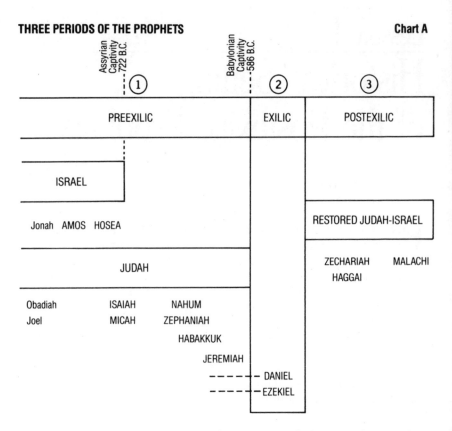

Because the books of the law are mostly historical records, they could be associated with the twelve books of history, making a total of seventeen historical books. In this simplified grouping, it is then correct to say that the Old Testament comprises history, poetry, and prophecy, in that order. Study Chart B, which shows these three groups.

Note the following on Chart B:

1. There is a general chronological progression in the books of history, from Genesis to Esther. (Read the top group from left to right.)

2. The poetry books, Job to Song of Solomon, revert back to a time earlier than the last three historical books.

3. The books of prophecy, from Isaiah to Malachi, cover a span of time that overlaps the history and poetry books and extends into the period of Ezra, Nehemiah, and Esther.

Chart B

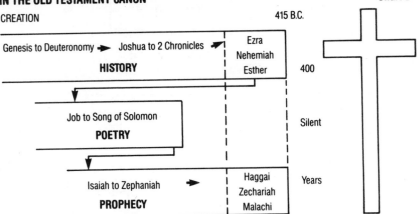

4. Ezra, Nehemiah, and Esther are chronologically the last historical records of the Old Testament. Haggai, Zechariah, and Malachi are chronologically the last prophetic messages of the Old Testament. Both groups are of the same time, which is the period of *restoration*. Record the word *restoration* in the appropriate blank box on the chart.

5. The period of 400 silent years is so named because no Scripture was written during this time. (Note that the number 400 is a round number.)

II. TWO KINGDOMS AND TWO CAPTIVES

Before we look at the restoration period of the postexilic prophets, let us review the historical setting *before* the restoration. When we speak of "restoration" we are referring to the conditions accompanying the *return* of God's people to Canaan *from captivity*. The captivity took place in two stages, known as the Assyrian and Babylonian captivities. See Chart C, which shows the two kingdoms of Israel and Judah and the two captivities.

A. Assyrian Captivity (fall of Samaria, 722 B.C., recorded in 2 Kings 17)

Most of the people and rulers of the ten tribes of the Northern Kingdom of Israel were deported to Assyria and scattered among the inhabitants there. The *Zondervan Pictorial Bible Dic-*

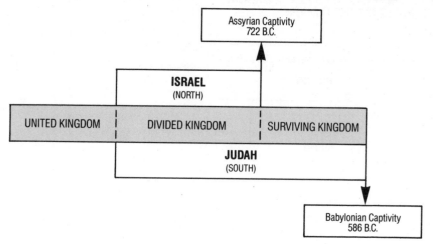

tionary comments on what happened to these people and their offspring in the years that followed:

> The Ten Tribes taken into captivity, sometimes called the Lost Tribes of Israel, must not be thought of as being absorbed by the people among whom they settled. Some undoubtedly were, but many others retained their Israelitish religion and traditions. Some became part of the Jewish dispersion, and others very likely returned with the exiles of Judah who had been carried off by Nebuchadnezzar.[3]

B. Babylonian Captivity (fall of Jerusalem, 586 B.C., recorded in 2 Kings 25)

The fall of Jerusalem in 586 B.C. sealed the fate of the two tribes of the Southern Kingdom of Judah. Nebuchadnezzar was the captor, and Babylon was the place of exile. Second Kings closes with an account of this tragic event in Judah's history. Read chapter 25 at this time to appreciate the theme of the restoration books. (Note: Unless otherwise stated, the names "Israel" and "Judah," denoting chosen people of God, will be used interchangeably throughout this manual.)

---

3. Merrill C. Tenney, ed., *The Zondervan Pictorial Bible Dictionary*, p. 147.

III. DURATION OF THE BABYLONIAN CAPTIVITY

Before Judah was taken captive, Jeremiah had prophesied that the duration of exile would be seventy years[4] (read Jer. 25:11-12; 29:10; 2 Chron. 36:21). The exile began with Nebuchadnezzar's first invasion of Judah in 605 B.C. (2 Chron. 36:2-7) and ended with the first return of the Jews to Canaan in 536 B.C.[5] (Ezra 1). See Chart D.[6]

IV. CONTEMPORARY RULERS

The Jews in exile in Babylonia were subject to the kings of the Neo-Babylonian Empire, such as Nebuchadnezzar. When Cyrus, king of Persia, overthrew Babylon in 539 B.C., the rule of Babylonia was transferred to the Persian Empire. Cyrus's policy of liberation for the exiles in Babylonia brought about the first return of Jewish exiles to the land of their fathers. Observe on Chart D the names of the Persian kings who succeeded Cyrus. The names of Darius and Artaxerxes appear frequently in the books of Ezra and Nehemiah. The former name appears three times in each of the books of Haggai and Zechariah.

V. LEADERS OF THE RESTORATION

Three key leaders of the returning Jews were Zerubbabel, Ezra, and Nehemiah. Zerubbabel and Nehemiah were appointed by Cyrus and Artaxerxes, respectively, as governors of the Jewish returnees. Ezra was a leading priest of the Jews who not only was a leader of the second return but also was a co-worker with Nehemiah on the third. Locate the names of Zerubbabel, Ezra, and Nehemiah on Chart D. Note also the dates associated with each of the three returns to Judah:

> 536 B.C.—first return under Zerubbabel
> 458 B.C.—second return under Ezra
> 445 B.C.—third return[7] under Nehemiah

---

4. Read Ezek. 36-48, which teaches that the Jews who would be returned to Canaan were to be gathered from many countries.
5. If Jeremiah's prophecy is interpreted from an ecclesiastical standpoint, with the Temple as the key object, then the seventy-year period extended from the destruction of the Temple in 586 B.C. to the year of completion of its reconstruction, which was in 516 B.C.
6. Most of the dates of Chart D are those of John C. Whitcomb's *Chart of Old Testament Kings and Prophets.*
7. No large contingent of Jews was involved in this return.

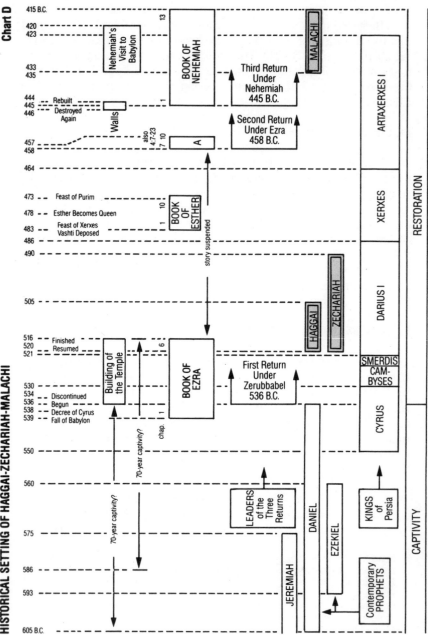

Chart D

HISTORICAL SETTING OF HAGGAI-ZECHARIAH-MALACHI

415 B.C.
420
423
Nehemiah's Visit to Babylon
13
BOOK OF NEHEMIAH
MALACHI
ARTAXERXES I
RESTORATION

433
435
Third Return Under Nehemiah 445 B.C.

444
445 — — Rebuilt
446 — — Destroyed Again
1
Walls

457 — — —
458 — — —
also 4:7-23
7 10
A
Second Return Under Ezra 458 B.C.

464

473 — — Feast of Purim
478 — — Esther Becomes Queen
483 — — Feast of Xerxes Vashti Deposed
486
490
10
BOOK OF ESTHER
1
XERXES

story suspended

505
ZECHARIAH
DARIUS I

516 — — Finished
520 — — Resumed
521
6
Building of the Temple
BOOK OF EZRA
HAGGAI

530
534 — — Discontinued
536 — — Begun
538 — — Decree of Cyrus
539 — — Fall of Babylon
First Return Under Zerubbabel 536 B.C.
SMERDIS
CAM-BYSES
CYRUS

1
chap.

70-year captivity?

550
560
LEADERS of the Three Returns
DANIEL
KINGS of Persia

70-year captivity?

575
EZEKIEL

586
593
JEREMIAH
Contemporary PROPHETS

605 B.C.

CAPTIVITY

12

Fix in your mind other dates and events cited on the chart. Refer back to this chart while you are studying the various lessons of this manual.

The preaching and teaching ministries of Haggai, Zechariah, and Malachi during the restoration period were crucial because they were God's messengers to the people. Observe on Chart D when these prophets ministered. Read Ezra 5:1 and 6:14 for brief but important mention of the influence of Haggai and Zechariah. The name *Malachi* does not appear in these or any other historical books. Observe on the chart that most of Malachi's ministry took place during Nehemiah's return visit to Babylon. Those were years of backsliding on the part of the Jews in Canaan, when the first spiritual zeal had subsided. Hence the message of Malachi was mainly about sin and its judgment.

The prophet Daniel went into exile with the first contingent of Jews in 605 B.C. and was ministering in Babylon in the services of Darius the Mede, who was made king of Babylon by Cyrus (Dan. 5:31, 9:1) when the exiles received permission to return (cf. Dan. 1:21, 6:28). Though aged Daniel did not return to Jerusalem with the exiles, he supported the project in spirit (see Dan. 9:1ff.).

VI. THREE PERIODS: KINGDOM, EXILE, RESTORATION

The Lord makes a clear diagnosis of Israel's spiritual condition during each of the three successive periods of kingdom, exile, and restoration, recorded in the book of Ezekiel. Read the verses cited on the work sheet of Chart E, and record in your own words the corresponding diagnosis:

In reading the above passages, did you observe these attributes of God:

1. God's holiness
2. God's justice—for example, sin brings judgment (cause-effect)
3. God's grace—for example, Ezekiel 36:22 (there would have been no restoration for Israel but for the grace of God)
4. God's omniscience and omnipotence—the only way to explain 36:23-32

VII. IMPORTANCE OF THE RESTORATION FOR THE JEWS AND THE WORLD

The restoration was important for various reasons. For Israel, it showed that God had not forgotten His promise to Abraham concerning the land of Canaan. (Read Gen. 13:15, and note the strength of the phrase "for ever"). Hence the *relocation* of a re-

13

PERIOD	REFERENCE IN EZEKIEL	SPIRITUAL CONDITION	
Kingdom 1043-586 B.C.	36:16-18		CAUSE
Exile 722-536 B.C.	36:19-21 2:3-7		EFFECT
Restoration 536-415 B.C.	36:22-32		SEQUEL

turning remnant. Hope for a missionary outreach for the Gentiles was stirred up in *revival* of true worship, for a key mission of Israel was to show the heathen nations of the world what true worship of the true God was. And then, the restoration was directly related to the life and ministry of the coming Messiah in the *renewal* of the messianic promises. For example, Bethlehem, Nazareth, and Zion were some of the geographical places woven into the promises concerning Jesus' coming. In about 400 years Jesus would be born of the seed of David in *Bethlehem, not* in Babylon. The Holy Land of *promise, not* a land of captivity, was where His people would be dwelling when He would come unto them, "His own" (John 1:11).

VIII. RESTORATION OF THE END TIMES

Israel's restoration in the sixth and fifth centuries B.C. was but a shadow of the final restoration in the messianic kingdom of the end times (Ezek. 36:22–37:28). By the time you read the last five verses of Ezekiel 37, you will realize that the prophecy concerns the still future messianic kingdom, with Christ ("David") ruling "for ever."

A prominent principle of Old Testament prophecy is that of multiple fulfillment. An example of this is Haggai 2:7, "I will fill this house with glory." This was a conditional prophecy about Zerubbabel's Temple, but more gloriously about the Temple of the messianic kingdom of the end times. Be ready to apply this principle of multiple fulfillment whenever you read a prophecy of restoration. For clear revelation that Israel will play a prominent role in world history of the end times, read Romans 11.

IX. THE MINISTRIES OF THE LAST THREE PROPHETS

See Chart D and note that Haggai and Zechariah ministered around the beginning of the restoration period, and Malachi ministered toward the end.[8] In the lessons that follow, more will be said about the immediate setting of the writing of each of their books. This may be noted now: the main appeal of Haggai and Zechariah was to inspire the Jews to finish building the Temple, which had been discontinued in 534 B.C. (Chart D); and the burden of Malachi was the tragic apostasy of God's people. Whatever there was of revival and spiritual restoration in Israel's return from exile had, by Malachi's time, degenerated to spiritual coldness with threat of disaster. It is not without significance that the last word of Malachi, and therefore of the Old Testament, is the awful word "curse." Read Malachi 4:6. What thoughts come to you as you compare this last verse with the Bible's first verse (Gen. 1:1)?

REVIEW QUESTIONS

1. What three historical books of the Bible record the last events of the Old Testament times?
2. What were the last three writing prophets to minister in Old Testament times?
3. When was the Northern Kingdom taken captive? When was the Southern Kingdom taken captive?
4. What two prophets ministered mainly to God's people in captivity after 586 B.C.?
5. Is it possible that descendants of Israelites of the Assyrian captivity were among the returning exiles from the Babylonian captivity?
6. What was the Lord's diagnosis of the spiritual condition of His people in each of the three periods of kingdom, exile, and restoration?

---

8. No historical event, as such, marks the end of the restoration period. The date 415 B.C. represents the last Old Testament historical record, given in Neh. 13. Note: During the restoration period the Jews were not ruled by kings but by governors appointed by a foreign king.

7. What does the word *restoration* suggest about Israel's experience?

8. According to Ezekiel 36:22-32, what was God's main purpose in leading His people back to Canaan?

9. Name three key leaders of the Jews when they returned to Canaan from Babylon.

10. In what different ways was the Jews' restoration important?

11. What did the restoration prefigure or typify?

12. What were the main spiritual burdens of Haggai, Zechariah, and Malachi?

Lesson 2
Background and Survey of Haggai

Haggai, one of the shortest Bible books, has been called a momentous Little fragment. Among its prominent teachings is the necessity of putting first things first. Who of us has not been guilty of violating this vital law of life?

Not long after God led the Jews out of exile back to Jerusalem, the people became self-satisfied and began to neglect the things of the Lord. They were building houses for themselves, but hardly a soul was grieved that the Temple building project, discontinued fourteen years earlier, remained at a standstill. To such a stagnant situation Haggai was sent with God's message. This lesson studies the background of that message and surveys the book that records it in our Bible.

I. BACKGROUND OF THE BOOK

Scan the book of Haggai before proceeding with this study of background.

A. The Man Haggai

Very little is known of the prophet Haggai. His name appears in two verses outside of his own book: Ezra 5:1; 6:14. Read these verses.

1. *Name.* The name *Haggai* means "festal" or "festive." We can only speculate why his parents gave him such a name. Did the name reflect their happy anticipation of returning to Jerusalem from exile? Was the baby Haggai born on a Jewish feast day? Was it the parents' divinely inspired hope that someday their son would be a messenger of happy news coming from God? Or did the

name simply reflect their sheer joy in having a son born to them? (The root of the word Haggai has the literal meaning of *celebration*. Read 1 Sam. 30:16, where the Hebrew word is translated "dancing.") Whatever led to the name, it was well chosen, for, as one writer has observed, "Haggai was one of the few prophets who had the inexpressible pleasure of seeing the fruits of his message ripen before his very eyes."[1]

2. *Home.* Haggai was probably born in Babylon during the captivity years. We know nothing about his family. He was among the first contingent of Jews returning to Jerusalem under the leadership of Zerubbabel (Ezra 2:2).

3. *Ministry.* The prophet Haggai is often referred to as "The Successful Prophet." No prophet saw a faster response to his message than he. Also, he has been called "the prophet who said it with bricks." This is because the main subject of his message was the completion of the Temple structure. Robert Lee writes, "Haggai stands before us as a model worker for God," shown in the following character study:

(a) He effaced himself. He spent no time giving details about his life and service. He exalted his Lord.
(b) He ever had a "thus saith the Lord." He was the Lord's messenger.
(c) He not only rebuked but cheered; not only criticized but commended and stimulated by word and example.
(d) He not only preached but practiced. He lent a hand (Ezra 5:1-2).[2]

Though Haggai's special ministry concerned the Temple project, he preached on other themes as well. Some of these will appear when we analyze the biblical text more closely.

Haggai and Zechariah were companions in the prophetic ministry. (See Chart D.) Read Ezra 5:1 and 6:14 again. How was the principle of co-working practiced in New Testament times? (Cf. Mark 6:7.) What are the advantages of a dual witness?

B. The Book of Haggai

1. *Date.* The book of Haggai clearly dates itself: "second year of Darius the king," which was 520 B.C. All four messages recorded in the book bear the same date as to year.

1. J. McIlmoyle, "Haggai," in *The New Bible Commentary,* p. 743.
2. See Robert Lee, *The Outlined Bible* (Westwood, N.J.: Revell, n.d.).

2. *Historical Setting.* As mentioned earlier, the Temple project is the focal issue of Haggai. The story of that project in the early years is a sad one indeed. To fully appreciate the prophet's burden, the following sequence of events, predating his writing, should be learned. (Read the Bible references, and locate some of the dates on Chart D.)

586 B.C. Jerusalem and the Temple are destroyed by the Babylonian invaders.

539 B.C. Babylon falls. The Persian Empire, ruled by King Cyrus, becomes a world power. The Jews in exile are now subject to Cyrus.

538 B.C. God moves Cyrus to issue a decree permitting and encouraging the Jews to return to their homeland (Ezra 1:1-4).

536 B.C. First return of Jews under Zerubbabel. Read Ezra 1:5–2:70 and Nehemiah 12. The total number of returnees: about 50,000. (See Ezra 2:64-67.)

536–535 B.C. Altar of burnt offerings is built at Jerusalem on the site of the Temple ruins. Feast of Tabernacles kept. Sacrifices observed (Ezra 3:1-6). Foundations of the Temple are laid (Ezra 3:7-13).

535-534 B.C. Opposition to Temple project by neighboring Samaritans (Ezra 4:1-5).

534 B.C. Work on Temple ceases[3] (Ezra 4:24).[4]

536-520 B.C. Israel's governor is Zerubbabel, who represents the king of Persia. Joshua the high priest is their religious leader.

520 B.C. Haggai and Zechariah begin to preach to the Jews in "Judah and Jerusalem in the name of the God of Israel" (Ezra 5:1; cf. Hag. 1:1). Temple project is resumed (Ezra 5:2; Hag. 1:14-15). For how many years had the people neglected the work?

516 B.C. Temple project is finished (Ezra 6:14-15).

Chart F shows the ever changing spiritual state of Israel during Old Testament times, and how Haggai's and Zechariah's ministries related to this.

---

3. Other factors besides the Samaritans' harassments caused the Jews to stop working on the Temple. Among these were (1) the people's earlier adjustment to worshiping without a temple when they were in Babylon; (2) their disillusionment upon returning to find mostly desolation, hostility, and hardship; (3) poverty resulting from failure of crops; and (4) preoccupation with their own building projects.

4. Verses 6-23 of chapter 4 are parenthetical, referring to the Samaritans' later opposition to building Jerusalem's walls during the reigns of Ahasuerus (486-464 B.C.) and Artaxerxes (464-423 B.C.)

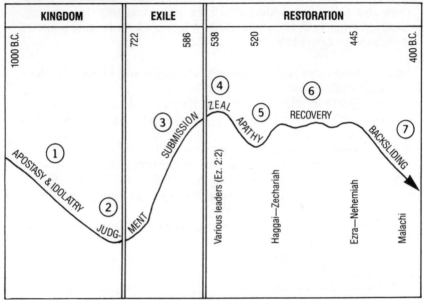

3. *The Importance of the Temple.* We may rightly ask why the Temple building was so crucial in the life of the Jews who had returned to Jerusalem. Gleason Archer suggests two basic reasons:

> It should be remembered that much of the Mosaic constitution presupposed the carrying on of worship in such a sanctuary, and the failure to complete a suitable house of worship could lead to a paralyzing of the religious life of the Jewish community. It should also be understood that the second temple was to play a very important role in the history of redemption, for it was in this temple (as remodeled and beautified by Herod the Great) that the Lord Jesus Christ was to carry on His Jerusalem ministry. It was, of course, His advent that fulfilled the promise of Haggai 2:9, "The glory of this latter house shall be greater than of the former."[5]

The Temple building itself, as a symbol, was intended to remind the Israelites that God was a real Person, alive, dwelling in Zion (Joel 3:21), and wanting to enjoy fellowship with man as well

5. Gleason L. Archer, *A Survey of Old Testament Introduction,* p. 408.

as to be worshiped by him. Exodus 25:8, referring to the original Tabernacle, gives clear insight into this fellowship aspect: "And, let them make me a sanctuary [*miqdash,* a place set apart], that I may dwell among them." There was no higher spiritual experience for a Jew in Haggai's time than by faith to let God as Lord dwell personally in his heart (cf. Acts 7:47-48; Isa. 66:1-2). In such an experience the Temple symbol bore its choicest eternal fruit.

4. *Theme of the Book.* The divine message that Haggai passed on to his Jewish brethren could have been summarized: "If you want to be restored to a blessed relationship with the Lord, put first things first in your life. For example, resume work on the Lord's Temple." This theme will be seen in more detail in the survey study later in the lesson.

5. *Names in the Book.* Four names important to the book are mentioned in its opening verse: Haggai the prophet; Darius the king; Zerubbabel the governor; and Joshua the high priest. Observe on Chart D the appearances of the first three names. Joshua (also called Jeshua) is listed in Ezra 2:2 as one of the leaders of the first return of exiles.

II. SURVEY OF HAGGAI

Before we analyze the individual verses of Haggai, survey the book as a whole. This follows the standard procedure of Bible study, "Image the whole, then execute the parts."

A. First Readings

1. First, mark paragraph divisions in your Bible beginning at these verses: 1:1, 3, 7, 12; 2:1, 10, 20.

2. Now read the whole book, rapidly. The purpose of this scanning is to see highlights, feel the tone, and register, at least mentally, some general impressions.

3. Scan the book again, with pencil in hand. Underline key repeated words and phrases as you read.

4. Did you notice various date references? Mark these in your Bible as 1:1, 1:15, 2:1, 2:10, 2:20.

5. At what places in the book does this group appear: Zerubbabel, Joshua, remnant? Does Haggai deliver a message to Zerubbabel only, at any place in the book?

B. Survey Chart

Chart G shows in layout form how the book of Haggai is or-

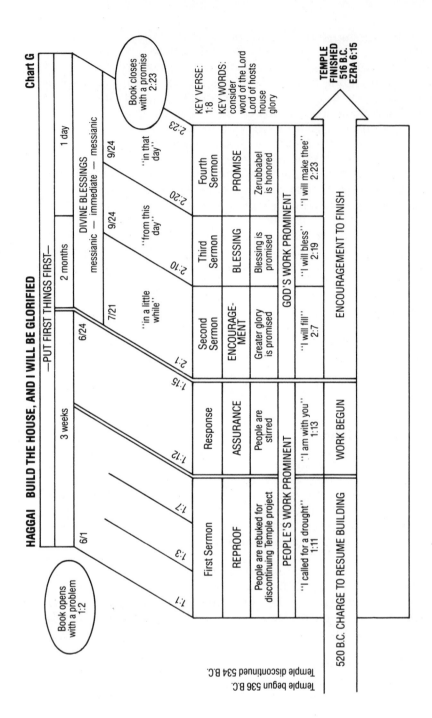

HAGGAI BUILD THE HOUSE, AND I WILL BE GLORIFIED

Chart G

—PUT FIRST THINGS FIRST—

Book opens with a problem 1:2

Book closes with a promise 2:23

	3 weeks	2 months	1 day
6/1	6/24	7/21	9/24	9/24

DIVINE BLESSINGS
messianic — immediate — messianic

| | 1:7 | 1:3 | 1:1 | 1:12 | 1:15 | 2:1 | 2:10 | 2:20 | 2:23 |

| | "in a little while" | "from this day" | "in that day" |

First Sermon	Response	Second Sermon	Third Sermon	Fourth Sermon
REPROOF	ASSURANCE	ENCOURAGE-MENT	BLESSING	PROMISE
People are rebuked for discontinuing Temple project	People are stirred	Greater glory is promised	Blessing is promised	Zerubbabel is honored
"I called for a drought" 1:11	"I am with you" 1:13	"I will fill" 2:7	"I will bless" 2:19	"I will make thee" 2:23

PEOPLE'S WORK PROMINENT ... GOD'S WORK PROMINENT

| | WORK BEGUN | ENCOURAGEMENT TO FINISH |

520 B.C. CHARGE TO RESUME BUILDING

Temple begun 536 B.C.
Temple discontinued 534 B.C.

TEMPLE FINISHED 516 B.C. EZRA 6:15

KEY VERSE:
1:8

KEY WORDS:
consider
word of the Lord
Lord of hosts
house
glory

22

ganized. Study this carefully as preparation for the analytical studies of lessons 3 and 4.

Note the following on the chart. (Check out the Bible references to justify the observations and outlines that appear on the chart.)

1. Note the title given to the book. See 1:8. Did you see many references to God's house when you scanned the text of Haggai? (An exhaustive concordance will quickly locate all of the references.)

2. Compare the book's opening (1:2) and closing (2:23).

3. Study the chronological sequence of the Temple project, beginning with the date 536 B.C. What three-part outline of Haggai relates to this?

4. How many "sermons" appear in the book? Check your Bible and note that each is dated. Note the dates recorded on the chart (e.g., 6/1). What is the total time span of the book?

5. What is the function of the short paragraph (1:12-15) between the first and second sermons?

6. Study the other outlines shown on the chart.

7. In what parts of Haggai do messianic prophecies appear?

8. Note the list of key words and phrases. Add to this list as you proceed with your analytical studies.

9. Use blank spaces on the chart for adding other outlines as you study.

REVIEW QUESTIONS

1. What does the name Haggai mean? Where was Haggai probably born? When did he first see the site of Jerusalem?

2. Who was Haggai's co-prophet?

3. When Haggai began his prophetic ministry, who was:
the Jews' governor?
the Jews' high priest?
Persia's king?

4. In what year did Haggai first preach the message recorded in his book?

5. Can you trace the spiritual state of Israel from 1000 B.C. to the time of Haggai's ministry?

6. Try to recall the key events of the Temple's history from 586 B.C. to 516 B.C. (70 years).

7. Why was the Temple building such an important object in the life of Israel?

8. What is the theme of the book of Haggai?

9. How many sermons are recorded in the book?

10. Quote at least part of the key verse, 1:8.

11. Can you recall one topical outline of the book of Haggai, as shown on the survey Chart G?

12. Haggai has been called "The Successful Prophet," and his writing has been called "The Book of Encouragement." Justify each of these.

"Build the House"

Chapter 1 of Haggai is the book's success story: A Prophet Preaches, and the People Respond. The story is brief, but the practical lessons it teaches are priceless. Every Christian can learn much from these fifteen verses.

I. PREPARATION FOR STUDY

1. Read Ezra 3:8–4:5 and 4:24 to review the setting of Haggai 1. Also keep in mind that building the Temple in Jerusalem had been the top-priority project for the returning exiles. Read Ezra 1:2-4.

2. Recall from your earlier studies that in the days of Haggai the Jews' immediate ruler was a governor appointed by Persia, not one of their own kings. This may help you see why a Temple building at this time would help restore a continuity with the nation's past. Of course, the purpose of the Temple had deep spiritual roots, as we saw in the last lesson.

II. ANALYSIS

Segment to be analyzed: 1:1-15
Paragraph divisions: at verses 1, 3, 7, 12 (Mark these in your Bible.)

A. The Segment as a Whole

1. Chart H is a work sheet for recording observations as you analyze the Bible text. You may want to prepare a similar work sheet on a sheet of paper (8½ x 11"). Examples of observations printed on Chart H are intended to show the kinds of things to look for in the text.

RESPONSE OF THE PEOPLE
HAGGAI 1:1-15

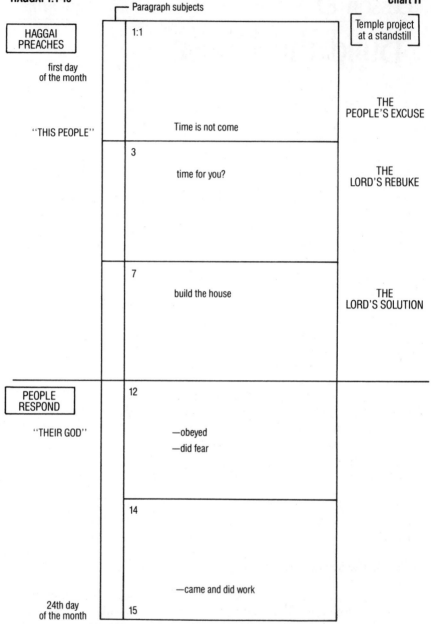

Paragraph subjects

HAGGAI
PREACHES

Temple project
at a standstill

first day
of the month

1:1

"THIS PEOPLE"

Time is not come

THE
PEOPLE'S EXCUSE

3

time for you?

THE
LORD'S REBUKE

7

build the house

THE
LORD'S SOLUTION

PEOPLE
RESPOND

12

"THEIR GOD"

—obeyed
—did fear

14

—came and did work

24th day
of the month

15

2. Read the chapter paragraph by paragraph, to determine the *main subject* of each. Record the subjects in the narrow boxes on the left-hand side.
3. Note that on Chart H paragraph 1:12-15 is set off from the first three paragraphs. Why?
4. Which paragraphs record mainly action, and which record mainly spoken words?
5. Read the segment again, underlining key words and phrases as you read. Record these on the analytical chart.
6. Compare the dates of 1:1 and 1:15. How much time transpired during the action of the chapter?
7. Note the dashed line shown at verse 14. Why is the paragraph divided at this point?
8. What are your general impressions of the chapter?

_____

_____

B. Paragraph by Paragraph

Use the work sheet of Chart H to record observations as you continue your study of the Bible text.
1. *The People's Excuse: 1:1-2*
Read 1:1. What four names of people are cited?

_____

_____

Compare their professions. How was each one involved with the people if Israel? From whom did Haggai receive a message?

_____

To whom was he to deliver the message?

_____

Is it implied by their very position that they were to pass on the message to the people? (Cf. vv. 2-4.)
Read 1:2. The Berkeley Version translates "The time is not come" as "The time has not yet come." What sin of Israel is the Lord condemning in this verse?

_____

Can you think of various excuses that the people may have given to justify waiting for what they would call the *right* time to go back to work on the Temple? Henrietta Mears comments that to Haggai

27

it must have "seemed incredible that God's people should have waited so long to do the very thing they came back to do."[1]

2. *The Lord's Rebuke: 1:3-6*

Read 1:3-4. Note how the Lord pursues the thought about "time," which the people had introduced, in verse 2. What sin is exposed in verse 4?

Read 1:5-6. What did the Lord mean by the words "Consider your ways"?

What was the people's plight, according to verse 6?

Does verse 6 indicate whether the plight was the *cause* of the people's neglect of the building program or the *consequence* of that neglect?

3. *The Lord's Solution: 1:7-11*

"No diagnosis without a cure." This is how we might describe God's grace-filled message throughout the Bible. Watch how the principle begins to show in this paragraph.

Read the five verses, observing how the subject changes as you move through the verses. That which appears to be a rambling of words without a pattern, on closer study shows an organized train of thought. The following outline suggests this. Check the outline with the Bible text.

SIN	God's house waste (**Cause**)	(1:4)
	People's plight (inferred as **Effect**)	(1:5-6)
CURE	— — — — — — — — — — — — — — — —	(1:7-8)
	People's plight (specified as **Effect**)	(1:9)
	People's plight further described	(1:10-11)

What was the divine cure for the people's problem, according to 1:8? Record this in your own words on the dashed line on the accompanying diagram.

Does 1:9 indicate whether the economic depression was the cause or effect of the people's neglect of the Temple?

1. Henrietta Mears, *What the Bible Is All About* (Glendale, Calif.: Gospel Light, 1953), p. 326.

4. *The People Respond: 1:12-15*

Do you see more of the Lord's gracious ways in this paragraph? Observe how the governor and high priest are identified with the people in verse 12. How is Haggai associated with the Lord in the same verse?

_____

_____

What two phrases record the people's response?

_____

_____

How is *obedience* related to the *fear* mentioned here?

_____

_____

How is Haggai identified in verse 13?

_____

_____

Do you think the Lord's message "I am with you" was the Lord's response to the people's obedience? In what sense had He been with them before their spiritual renewal of 1:12?

_____

Read 1:14-15. Record the facts of these verses:
WHO:

_____

WHAT:

_____

WHEN:

_____

How do you suppose the Lord "stirred up the spirit" of the rulers and the people?

_____

Why was it vital that *both* groups be stirred up?

_____

_____

Compare the phrases:
       "the Lord of hosts, their God"   (1:14)
       "Darius the king"   (1:15)

Do you think the people's involvement in the Temple project could help them direct their sights more to God and away from human leaders?

Compare the time references of 1:1 and 1:15. How many days transpired between Haggai's first preaching to the people and their working on the Temple?

III. NOTES

1. *"Word of the Lord"* (1:1). Divine authority of Haggai's message is prominent throughout the book. Someone has observed that in at least twenty-five of the book's thirty-eight verses this authority is either implied or explicitly stated.

2. *"Joshua"* (1:1). The phrase "the high priest" in this verse is intended to modify the name of Joshua. *The Living Bible* reads, "And Joshua (son of Josedech), the High Priest."

3. *"Lord of hosts"* (1:2). This common title of Jehovah appears first in the Bible as 1 Samuel 1:3. Who do you think the hosts are? (Cf. Ex. 12:41.)

4. *"This people"* (1:2). The phrase suggests estrangement. Compare "My people" (Hos. 2:23). A backslidden believer is out of fellowship with his Lord.

5. *"The time is not come"* (1:2). It is unlikely that the people meant by this that the seventy-year[2] captivity was not yet complete (since 586 B.C. minus 70 years = 516 B.C.) and that therefore the Temple project could be postponed for even longer.

6. *"Ceiled houses"* (1:4). The walls and ceilings of such houses were wood-paneled, an expensive luxury in Canaan.

7. *"Consider your ways"* (1:5). The word "consider" means literally "set your heart to." The exhortation in Haggai is to ponder, evaluate, take inventory (cf. 1:7; 2:15, 18).

8. *"Mine house that is waste"* (1:9). "Waste" may be translated "in ruins." The Hebrew word is *chareb*. There seems to be a play on words when the Lord, a little later, says, "I called for a drought [Heb., *choreb*]" (1:11).

IV. FOR THOUGHT AND DISCUSSION

1. We hear much today about authority and freedom. What is absolute authority? Is the Word of God absolute authority? What is meant by a Christian's being a bondslave of Jesus Christ?

2. Jeremiah had clearly prophesied a seventy-year period (see Jer. 25:11).

2. Did you learn any practical lessons about procrastination in this chapter? What are your thoughts about "time" as the word is used in 1:2 and 1:4?

3. Why is a local church building, when truly devoted as the Lord's house, an important *ingredient* of Christianity? Compare this with the Temple of Old Testament times.

4. What are your thoughts about priorities in the Christian life? See Matthew 6:33.

5. When God sends or permits financial setback to a believer, what may be His purpose?

6. Why is obedience to God the key to being in His will?

7. What do the words of God "I am with you" mean to you? Read these verses where the assuring promise of the Lord's presence is recorded: Exodus 3:12; Jeremiah 1:8; Matthew 28:20.

8. Does the Christian church need to be stirred up today? Is this one of the present ministries of the Holy Spirit in Christians? (Cf. 2 Pet. 1:13; 3:1.)

9. What does Haggai 1 teach about how a believer's works are related to his heart?

V. FURTHER STUDY

1. The name "God" (Heb., *Elohim*) appears only three times in Haggai (1:12, 14). The name "Lord" (*Jehovah*) appears thirty times. The name *Elohim* signifies Creator, whereas the name *Jehovah* essentially means Saviour. Study the context of 1:12 and 1:14 to see how and why the two names are brought together.

2. Study what the New Testament teaches about the ministries of the Holy Spirit in this present age. Included among these are regeneration, sanctification, baptism, indwelling, sealing, filling, instruction, conviction. Two main sources for help in such a study are a book of Christian doctrine and a topical work such as John F. Walvoord's *The Holy Spirit.*[3]

VI. WORDS TO PONDER

You hope for much but get so little.... Why? Because my Temple lies in ruins and you don't care (Hag. 1:9, *The Living Bible*).

---

3. John F. Walvoord, *The Holy Spirit* (Grand Rapids: Zondervan, 1954).

"I Will Fill This House with Glory"

In Haggai chapter 1 the prominent subject is the people's return to work on the Temple project. Now the remainder of the book (chap. 2) is about God's work on behalf of His people, not only those of Haggai's time but also of the generations to come. Three key phrases in the chapter bear this out: "I will fill"; "I will bless"; "I will make." Chapter 2 is another page of Scripture demonstrating the amazing grace of God. How else can one describe the long-suffering of God with people who so quickly grow cold and spurn His fellowship?

I. PREPARATION FOR STUDY

1. Compare the time references of 1:15 and 2:1. For how many days had the Jews been working on the Temple when Haggai delivered the Lord's message of 2:3-9 to them?

2. Read Haggai 2:3, noting the phrase "this house in her first glory." The reference is to Solomon's Temple, which had been destroyed in 586 B.C. Read the Bible's description of Solomon's Temple in 2 Chronicles 2:1–7:22. The building had been noted more for its exquisite beauty than for its size.

3. Review what you learned in Lesson 1 about the restoration of Israel in the end times. Recall what is meant by the prophetic principle of multiple fulfillment. Chart I shows how one prediction of an Old Testament prophet like Haggai could refer to three widely separated "kingdoms" of God's people (A, B, C).

4. Read Hebrews 12:25-29, noting the references to the Lord's judgments of shaking.

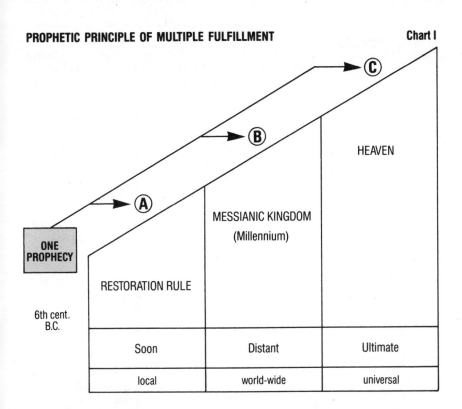

II. ANALYSIS

Segment to be analyzed: 2:1-23
Paragraph divisions: at verses 2:1, 10, 20

A. The Segment as a Whole

1. Scan the chapter for overall impressions.
2. Chart J is a partially completed analytical chart showing the main structural relations of the three paragraphs of this segment. Use the chart as a work sheet to record other observations as you study.
3. Note on the chart that each of Haggai's three sermons are dated. See 2:1, 10, 20.
4. Note how the prophecies of the first and third sermons are similar to each other. Read 2:6-9 and 2:21-23. You will want to come to a decision as to what time or times the Lord intended the prophecies to be fulfilled. (Refer to Chart I.) Consider the following seven possible interpretations:

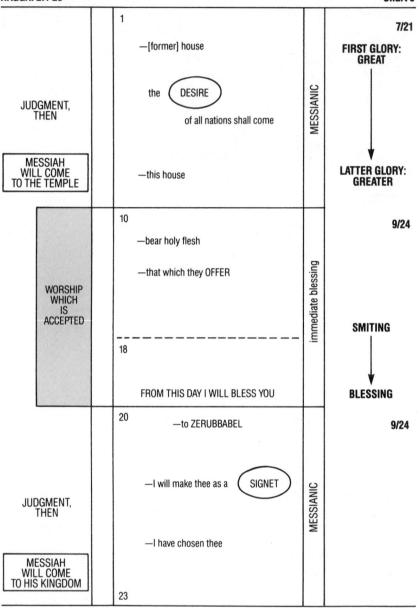

	1	7/21
	—[former] house	**FIRST GLORY:** **GREAT**
JUDGMENT, THEN	the (DESIRE)	MESSIANIC
	of all nations shall come	
MESSIAH WILL COME TO THE TEMPLE	—this house	**LATTER GLORY:** **GREATER**
	10	9/24
	—bear holy flesh	
WORSHIP WHICH IS ACCEPTED	—that which they OFFER	immediate blessing
	18	**SMITING**
	FROM THIS DAY I WILL BLESS YOU	**BLESSING**
	20	9/24
	—to ZERUBBABEL	
JUDGMENT, THEN	—I will make thee as a (SIGNET)	MESSIANIC
	—I have chosen thee	
MESSIAH WILL COME TO HIS KINGDOM	23	

34

a. to be fulfilled not long after Haggai preached
b. to be fulfilled in a far-distant messianic kingdom
c. to be fulfilled in heaven, at the end of time
d. two fulfillments: (1) and (2) above
e. two fulfillments: (1) and (3) above
f. two fulfillments: (2) and (3) above
g. three fulfillments: (1), (2), and (3) above

Keep these different interpretations in mind as you analyze the paragraph more closely, and decide which option is best supported by the Bible text.[1]

5. A key word of the first paragraph is "desire" (2:7). A key word of the third paragraph is "signet" (2:3). Circle these words in your Bible.

6. Later in the lesson we will see that the second sermon concerned the *immediate future*. A key subject of this middle paragraph is *worship* (left-hand margin).

B. Paragraph by Paragraph

1. *The Desire of All Nations: 2:1-9*
Read 2:1-3. What comparison does the Lord make in verse 3?

_____

Do the words suggest that already, three weeks after returning to work (1:14-15), the people are getting discouraged? Is such discouragement and disenchantment suggested by 2:4-5? Note the key exhortations: "Be strong...work...fear not." Do you think the words "her first glory (2:3) may have referred more to spiritual glory than to architectural beauty? Recall what God had said earlier to the people about the Temple He wanted them to rebuild: "I will be glorified" (1:8). While the Jews were working on Zerubbabel's Temple, some of their elders apparently were expressing their gloom that this Temple would never have the spiritual associations with history that Solomon's Temple had. For example, as claimed by one ancient nonbiblical writing,[2] five things were lacking that had been in Solomon's Temple: (1) the Shekinah glory; (2) the holy fire; (3) the Ark of the Covenant; (4) the Urim and Thummim; and (5) the spirit of prophecy. What did the elders and

---

1. The seven options noted here appear in the study of many Old Testament prophecies. Multiple fulfillments of prophecy are common in the Old Testament.
2. See *The Wycliffe Bible Commentary*, p. 891, for this Talmudic citation.

the people need to be reminded of concerning the real purpose and destiny of the Temple? (That counsel is recorded in 2:6-9.)

Read 2:6-7. Note the appearances of the key words "glory" and "peace." If Haggai's audience took the Lord's promises to be about the immediate future, how would their discouragement and fear noted above be alleviated?

If the prophecies of 2:6-9 predicted a soon fulfillment (e.g., within the next 100 years), how would these descriptions apply:
"I will shake all nations" (2:7).
"The desire of all nations shall come" (2:7). (See *Notes.*)
"I will fill this house with glory" (2:7).
Now interpret 2:6-9 as referring to the end times, centered about the Person of Christ as Messiah. Such an interpretation would involve the following: First will come the Tribulation (note the repeated word "shake"). See Revelation 16:18-20 and 19:11-21 for two descriptions of such judgment. At the end of the Tribulation, Christ, the "desire of all nations," will come to rule and be worshiped in His house.[3] See Revelation 20:1-6 for a brief account of the millennial reign of Christ. Why would the binding of Satan support the setting of glory and peace prophesied in Haggai 2:6-9?

Compare the prophecies of Isaiah 2:2-4 and Zechariah 8:21-23; 14:16.
In what ways will heaven be the perfect fulfillment of conditions described in 2:6-9? (Cf. Rev. 21.)

How is the temple of heaven identified in Revelation 21:22?

2. *Worship that is accepted: 2:10-19*
See how this paragraph is represented on Chart J.

3. Regardless of how the word "desire" is interpreted, the coming of Christ still fits this eschatological application of 2:6-9.

Read 2:10-14. What do the verses teach about the kind of worship and devotion accepted by God?

_____

_____

Why is true, dynamic worship of God a foundation condition for divine blessing in His Kingdom?

_____

_____

Read 2:15-19. Had Haggai preached the message of verses 15-17 in earlier sermons? How do the verses lead into the main point of 2:18-19?

_____

_____

What is the strong promise of 2:18-19?

_____

_____

Is this related in any way to the prophecy of 2:6-9?

_____

_____

3. A *Signet: 2:20-23*
Read 2:20-21*a*. Note that this message is given only to Zerubbabel (cf. 2:2). Why? (See v. 23.)

_____

_____

What message is repeated in 2:22 that appeared in an earlier sermon?

_____

Does this suggest that both prophecies may relate to the same time?
Read 2:23. Who is the object of these prophecies?

_____

_____

What do you think is meant by the words, "I . . . will make thee as a signet"? (See *Notes*.)

_____

In this connection, read Genesis 38:18; Exodus 28:11; and Jeremiah 22:24, where the same Hebrew word for "signet" is used. Whatever the exact meaning, Haggai's prophecy is a bright one. Suppose you were Zerubbabel listening to the prophecy of 2:23 about yourself. How might you interpret the promise, since no specific details are given in it?

Today as we look back on history, we observe that no unusual or spectacular honor came to Governor Zerubbabel during his lifetime.[4] As Hobart Freeman points out, "Zerubbabel never at any time reigned upon the throne of David in Jerusalem over the subdued kingdoms of the world."[5] This points to the fact that the prophecy of 2:23 had a more *distant* fulfillment view (cf. Heb. 11:13). The question that comes to us immediately is: Was there an intended association between Zerubbabel and Christ, whether in type, symbol, or even ancestry? In connection with the latter, read Luke 3:27 and observe that Zerubbabel was an ancestor of Christ. Charles Feinberg writes:

> The promise actually pertains to the office Zerubbabel filled as ruler in Judah; it cannot refer to Zerubbabel's own lifetime. In his day the predicted events did not transpire. The meaning is that the messianic descent was to come through Zerubbabel, of the line of David. . . . David's secure throne is here contrasted with the tottering dynasties of the world.[6]

As a messianic prophecy, how is 2:23 an appropriate conclusion to the entire book of Haggai?

_____

_____

Recall the Zerubbabel was "only" the governor of Judah, subject to King Darius. Compare this office with that of Jesus Christ, King of kings (Rev. 19:16).

III. NOTES

1. *"Who . . . saw this house in her first glory?"* (2:3). The last time anyone had seen the Temple was in the year of its destruction, 586 B.C., or sixty-six years earlier. Even a young teenager who

---

4. In an apocryphal book—Ecclesiasticus, which was written some 300 years after Haggai—Zerubbabel is listed among the heroes of Israel, but the eulogy does not add anything not written in Haggai (Ec'us 49:11).
5. Hobart E. Freeman, *An Introduction to the Old Testament Prophets,* p. 332.
6. Charles L. Feinberg, "Haggai," in *The Wycliffe Bible Commentary,* p. 895.

had left in 586 B.C. with the conquered Jews would now be at least eighty years old.

2. *"The word that I covenanted with you when ye came out of Egypt"* (2:5). Read Exodus 19:5-6 for a brief wording of this post-Egypt covenant made at Sinai.

3. *"Yet once, it is a little while"* (2:6). This reads better as, "Once more in a little while" (NASB; Berkeley).

4. *"I will shake all nations"* (2:7). Those who interpret the predictions of 2:7 to happen before Christ's first advent see the fulfillment of the shaking in the conquests of the kingdoms of Persia, Greece, and Rome in the centuries before Christ.

5. *"The desire of all nations shall come"* (2:7). The Hebrew word translated "shall come" is plural, whereas the word translated "desire" is singular. This is partly the reason for the following translations: "the precious things of all nations shall come" (ASV); "the wealth of all nations shall come" (Berkeley note). The suggestion of these translations is that Gentile nations would have a part in God's purpose for Israel by bringing their treasures to Him (returning God's silver and gold to Him, 2:8.) The footnote of the *Amplified Bible* says:

> The verb "shall come" is plural, and, as many commentators agree, refers to the most desired treasures that all nations will bring as gifts to adorn the temple to which the Messiah will one day have come. Thus the Messianic reference of the prophecy is neither questioned not obscured, but the picture presented is like that of the coming of the Magi to find the Babe of Bethlehem, the Desire of all of them; and when they found Him they fell down and worshipped Him, bringing Him their most desirable treasures, gold, frankincense and myrrh.

In support of the view that a person, the Messiah, is intended by the word "desire" are these factors:

a. This was the interpretation of most of the early Christian expositors.

b. Jewish tradition has always identified the Messiah with the word "Desire."

c. Christ is the desire of all nations in the sense that they yearn "for the Deliverer, whether or not they realize the nature of their desire or the identity of its true fulfillment in the Lord Jesus Christ."[7]

---

7. See *The Wycliffe Bible Commentary*, p. 893.

d. The use of a plural verb does not necessarily rule out interpreting "desire" as a single person.[8]

e. If 2:6-9 is messianic, it is natural that a reference to the Messiah appears someplace in the passage.

f. Other prophecies (i.e., Zech. 6:9-15) clearly relate Christ to the Temple. (Note the messianic symbol "Branch" in Zech. 6:12.)

6. *"Holy flesh"* (2:12). The flesh was meat, sanctified by having been offered in sacrifice to God.

7. *"I . . . will make thee as a signet"* (2:23). A signet ring was often a seal of a pledge (cf. Gen. 38:18; Jer. 22:24). It was also "a mark of honor, a badge of royal authority possessed by kings and conferred on their administrative agents."[9] J. Sidlow Baxter comments on this beautiful messianic prophecy:

> In the last great victory of the Divine purpose, Christ, the greater Son and wonderful Antitype of David and Zerubbabel, will be Jehovah's signet whereby He shall impress and imprint upon all nations His own majesty, His own will and ways, His own perfect ideal, and His own very image.[10]

IV. FOR THOUGHT AND DISCUSSION

1. When will true and lasting peace come to this world, if ever? Why has not man seen this kind of peace yet?

2. Is unholiness communicable (2:13-14)? How can a Christian guard himself from the defilement of worldly things? Is holiness communicable (2:12)? In what sense can a Christian's good witness influence others?

3. What part does God play in the affairs of nations today? Why does He permit evil nations to continue? How will the last chapter of world history read?

4. "Promises are often made to individuals in Scripture which only find fulfillment in their descendants."[11] Was it unethical of God not to give dates of fulfillment in His prophetic messages? Why such silence on dates?

5. "Zerubbabel himself may share as one of Messiah's prime ministers in the kingdom."[12] What are your thoughts about the kinds of ministries that believers will have in the millennial Kingdom and in heaven? (Cf. Matt. 19:28; Rev. 22:3.)

8. Ibid.
9. Merrill F. Unger, *Unger's Bible Handbook,* p. 434.
10. J. Sidlow Baxter, *Explore the Book,* 4:234. Definition: An antitype is that to which a type points, the fulfillment of that kind of prophecy.
11. Hobart E. Freeman, *An Introduction to the Old Testament Prophets,* p. 332.
12. Merrill F. Unger, *Unger's Bible Handbook,* p. 434.

6. Why was the Temple such an important object in the life of Israel? Relate 1 Peter 2:5 to this, as involving Christians.

7. What spiritual lessons have stood out as prominent in your study of Haggai? Can you apply any of these to your own life?

8. Apply these teachings of Haggai about work to the unfinished task of the church:[13]

a. The Lord's work takes priority over every other obligation.

b. Those who obey God and work, trusting in His abiding presence and power, are kept from discouragement.

c. The Lord's work demands clean instruments, separated from sin.

d. The Lord's work, believingly carried on, is linked to His sovereign plan for men and nations.

V. FURTHER STUDY

Study the subject *temple* in a Bible dictionary or Bible encyclopedia. Concentrate especially on Zerubbabel's Temple and its replacement by Herod's Temple, which was still being built during Jesus' public ministry (John 2:20).

VI. WORDS TO PONDER

Be strong . . . and work: for I am with you, saith the Lord of hosts (Hag. 2:4).

Therefore, my beloved brethren, be ye steadfast, unmovable, always abounding in the work of the Lord, forasmuch as ye know that your labour is not in vain in the Lord (1 Cor. 15:58).

---

13. From Frank E. Gaebelein, *Four Minor Prophets,* p. 244.

Lesson 5
Background and Survey of Zechariah

Zechariah, the longest book of the Minor Prophets, is often quoted in the New Testament. This is because so many of its prophecies point forward to Christ the Messiah. One Bible scholar has called Zechariah "the most Messianic, the most truly apocalyptic and eschatological, of all the writings of the Old Testament."[1]

Visions, symbols, and prophecies of the end times (eschatology) abound in Zechariah. These are the main ingredients of apocalyptic literature (Gk. *apokalupsis*, meaning "uncovering," "disclosure," "revelation"). This is why the book is often referred to as "The Book of Revelation of the Old Testament." As such it is appropriate that the book appear toward the end of the Christian canon of the Old Testament (next to the last book).

In this lesson we will first study the background of the writing of the book and then survey its pages in a general way to grasp the overall theme and structural pattern. This will be good preparation for the analytical studies that follow.

For now, before you move to the background studies, spend fifteen minutes scanning the book in a modern paraphrase like *The Living Bible*. This will help attach some personality to the book and remove it from the "stranger" classification.

I. BACKGROUND OF THE BOOK OF ZECHARIAH

A. The Man Zechariah

1. *Name.* The Hebrew name *Zechariah* means "The Lord remembers." It was a common name in Old Testament times; about thirty men in the Old Testament are so named. Many parents no

---

1. George L. Robinson, "The Book of Zechariah," in *The International Standard Bible Encyclopedia* 5:3136.

doubt gave the name as an act of gratitude to the Lord for remembering them with the gift of a baby boy.

2. *Family*. Zechariah's father was the priest Berechiah; his grandfather, priest Iddo (1:1).[2] Zechariah's family was among the Jewish exiles who returned from Babylon in 536 B.C. under Zerubbabel. (Read Neh. 12:4, 16.) Zechariah was a young child at that time if he was a young man when he began to prophesy in 520 B.C. (The "young man" of 2:4 may be Zechariah.)

3. *Ministry*. In 520 B.C., when God began revealing to Haggai the message he should preach and write, Zechariah was ministering to the Jews as a priest, a position passed down from his forefathers (Neh. 12:16). Then, two months later, Zechariah was commissioned with a similar prophetic task (cf. Hag. 1:1; Zech. 1:1). This made him a prophet-priest like his predecessors Jeremiah and Ezekiel. Jewish tradition honors Zechariah (along with Haggai and Malachi) as a priest of the Great Synagogue, responsible for gathering and preserving the sacred writings and traditions of the Jews after the Babylonian exile.

The main task Zechariah and Haggai shared was to exhort the Jews to finish rebuilding the Temple. This project had been discontinued in 534 B.C., fourteen years before the prophets began their ministry. Read Ezra 6:14-15 to learn how successful the prophets were. In what year was the Temple completed?

The question is sometimes asked if there was needless duplication in the ministries of Zechariah and Haggai. The answer is negative, for various reasons. One writer points out that Haggai's chief task was to rouse the people to the *outward* task of building the Temple, whereas Zechariah kept urging the people to examine their hearts and be right with God.[3] It was a difference of emphasis only. Another difference was that Zechariah preached a great deal about the messianic Kingdom of the end times. God revealed this information to him through a series of apocalyptic visions (cf. Zech. 1:8, 18 and Rev. 1:9-11). How soon did the visions begin after God first gave him the prophetic message? (Cf. 1:1 and 1:7.)

B. The Book of Zechariah

1. *Date*. There are datelines in Zechariah at 1:1; 1:7; and 7:1.

2. Ezra 5:1 says Zechariah was a son of Iddo. In Jewish terminology, "son of" had the wider designation of "descendant of." It is possible that Berechiah died before Iddo, causing Ezra to identify Zechariah with the surviving ancestor of the priestly line.
3. David Baron, *The Visions and Prophecies of Zechariah* (London: Hebrews Christian Testimony, 1951), p. 9.

The second year of Darius (1:1) was 520 B.C., and the fourth year (7:1) was 518 B.C. The opening words of 8:1 suggest a later revelation to Zechariah, as do the opening words of 9:1. How much later these revelations were given, however, cannot be determined. It is possible that chapters 1-8 were written during the building of the Temple (520 B.C.); and chapters 9-14, after the Temple was completed in 516 B.C. (See Chart K.)

2. *General Contents.* Like all biblical prophecy, the Zechariah contains both foretelling and forthtelling. The forthtelling is the prophet's appeal to the people concerning their *heart* relationship to God, so that the work of their *hands* (e.g., Temple project) might prosper. The foretelling concerns Israel's fortunes and judgments in the years to come, culminating in the nation's glory when the Messiah would come. Such predictions were intended to make the Jews yearn to see their King.

3. *Main Purposes.* Four purposes of the book may be cited:

a. To bring about spiritual revival. What was the first message of the Lord to the Jews? See 1:2-3.

b. To inspire the people to complete the Temple building. See 1:16 and 4:9 for two specific references to the Temple.

c. To comfort and console the people. See 1:13. The Jews were going through severe trials at this time. (This background was studied in Lesson 2.)

d. To register in divine Scripture unmistakable prophecies about the coming Messiah. The fact that the Jews hearing Zechariah's prophecies did not live to see the fulfillment did not detract from the intended inspiration of the prophecies to their souls. (Cf. 1 John 3:2-3.)

There are more prophecies of Christ in Zechariah than in any other prophetic book except Isaiah. Underline these in your Bible now. (The list of verses about fulfillment is a partial list.)

PROPHECY OF CHRIST		FULFILLMENT
Servant	3:8	Mark 10:45
Branch	3:8; 6:12	Luke 1:78
King-Priest	6:13	Heb. 6:20-7:1
Lowly King	9:9-10	Matt. 21:4-5; John 12:14-16
Betrayed	11:12-13	Matt. 27:9
Hands pierced	12:10	John 19:37
Cleansing fountain	13:1	Rev. 1:5
Humanity and deity	13:7; 6:12	John 8:40; 1:1
Smitten shepherd	13:7-9	Matt. 26:31; Mark 14:27
Second coming and coronation	14:5, 9	John 10:16; Rev. 11:15; 21:27

II. SURVEY OF THE BOOK OF ZECHARIAH

1. First, mark in your Bible the twenty units shown on Chart K. That is, draw a line across the page of your Bible at 1:1; 1:7; 1:18, etc. (Note: The units of chaps. 1-8 are paragraphs; those of 9-14 are full chapters.)

2. Now scan the entire book with pencil in hand. Note especially the opening verse of each of the twenty units. Underline any key words and phrases that strike you.

3. Study Chart K. Note that the chart divides the book into three main divisions. What are they?

4. How does the paragraph 1:1-6 introduce the book? Is there a formal conclusion to the book?

5. Note where the eight visions are recorded. Read each of these visions in the Bible text to justify the titles shown on the chart. Note how the words "saw," "looked," or "eyes" introduce the visions.

6. Read 6:9-15. The absence of sight words is the reason for not identifying this passage as a vision. How is this paragraph a fitting conclusion to the divine revelation of chapters 1-6?[4] Compare the last words of 6:15 with 1:3.

7. Note on Chart K the middle section called *four messages*. Read in your Bible the four verses cited on the chart. What common phrase introduces each of the messages?

8. Chapters 9-14 are identified as *two burdens*. Read 9:1 and 12:1 for the origin of this title.

9. Note on the chart that the ten oblique spaces representing 7:1 to the end of the book are blank. Use these spaces to record titles as you proceed with your studies in later lessons. Also, use the large area at the bottom of the entire chart to record other outlines that may come to you later.

10. At this time you need not try to justify the outlines shown on the chart involving chapters 9-14. This will be done in Lesson 8.

11. Note the title assigned to the book of Zechariah shown at the top of the chart. Compare this with the key verses. Also note the key words. You will probably want to add to this list in your later studies.

12. Refer back to this survey chart during your analytical studies. This will help you keep the context in mind.

---

4. Recall from 1:1 that all of chapters 1-6 was revealed to Zechariah "in the eighth month, in the second year of Darius."

ZECHARIAH KING OVER ALL THE EARTH

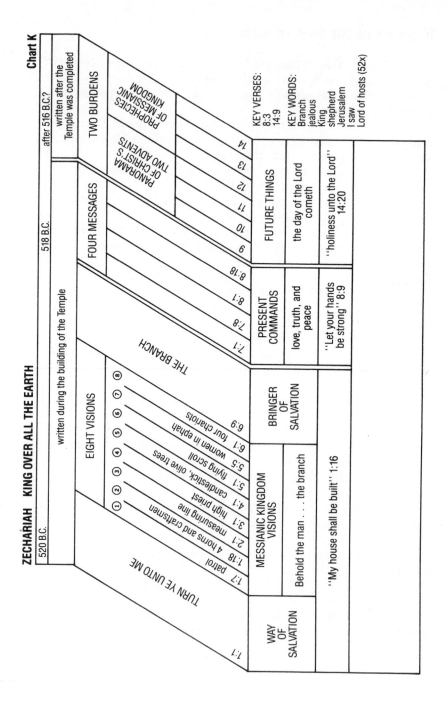

Chart K

520 B.C.	518 B.C.	after 516 B.C.?
written during the building of the Temple		written after the Temple was completed
EIGHT VISIONS	FOUR MESSAGES	TWO BURDENS

TURN YE UNTO ME | THE BRANCH

Visions:
① 1:7 patrol
② 2:1 4 horns and craftsmen
③ 3:1 measuring line / high priest
④ 4:1 candlestick, olive trees
⑤ 5:1 flying scroll
⑥ 5:5 women in ephah
⑦ 6:9 four chariots
⑧

FOUR MESSAGES: 7:1 · 7:8 · 8:1 · 8:18

PANORAMA OF CHRIST'S TWO ADVENTS — 9 10 11 12 13 14

PROPHECIES OF MESSIANIC KINGDOM

WAY OF SALVATION	MESSIANIC KINGDOM VISIONS	BRINGER OF SALVATION	PRESENT COMMANDS	FUTURE THINGS
	Behold the man . . . the branch		love, truth, and peace	the day of the Lord cometh
"My house shall be built" 1:16			"Let your hands be strong" 8:9	"holiness unto the Lord" 14:20

KEY VERSES:
8:3
14:9

KEY WORDS:
Branch
jealous
King
shepherd
Jerusalem
I saw
Lord of hosts (52x)

46

REVIEW QUESTIONS

1. What does the name Zechariah mean? How old a man was Zechariah when he began to prophesy?
2. In what position was Zechariah serving when God's prophetic call came to him?
3. Compare Zechariah's ministry with Haggai's. Why were two prophets serving at the same time?
4. What is known about Zechariah's death?
5. What dates can be assigned to the book of Zechariah? What about chapters 9-14 as to date?
6. What are the main purposes of the book?
7. How many chapters are there in Zechariah?
8. What are the three main divisions in the book?
9. Can you quote a key verse of Zechariah?
10. List some key words of the book.

A CONCLUDING THOUGHT

As you have been studying about Old Testament prophets like Zechariah and Haggai, has it occurred to you that all Christians have a special place and ministry in this world, sovereignly appointed by God, and no less important than the ministry of the prophets? Read 1 Corinthians 12. Is it your earnest desire to be used of God *as He will*?

Zechariah's Night Visions

Zechariah was one of the few Bible authors to whom God gave extended visions about things to come. As noted earlier, his writing is sometimes called "The Book of Revelation of the Old Testament." The eight visions recorded in chapters 1-6 came one night soon after the prophet had begun preaching (1:7-8).

The visions were the Lord's way of impressing upon the prophet the vivid reality of the events symbolized. The prophet was always at a loss to interpret the symbols; but every time he inquired about their meaning, he was given an answer. In this lesson we will study the visions and their meanings, and we will want to learn how the visions were meant to be applied. In other words, our study will involve the three areas of observation, interpretation, and application.

I. PREPARATION FOR STUDY

1. Keep in mind as you study this and the following three lessons that Zechariah's ministry was closely related to Haggai's. It was Haggai who had built up a momentum in the Temple project, and now Zechariah was sent to strengthen that momentum with spiritual forces. Chart L shows how the ministries of the two prophets overlapped. Study the chart carefully. Read each of the Bible references. They are the sources for the time spans shown on the chart.[1]

2. Various things should be kept in mind when you study the apocalyptic visions of Zechariah. Among these are:

---

1. No dateline is given by 9:1. Chapters 9-14 were possibly written after the completion of the Temple project, though this cannot be supported by any specific data. Recall the survey Chart K.

THE OVERLAPPING MINISTRIES OF HAGGAI AND ZECHARIAH

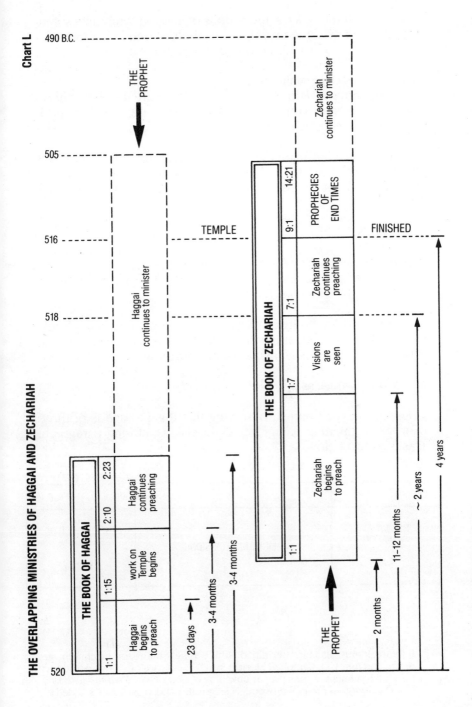

Chart L

THE PROPHET

Zechariah continues to minister

490 B.C.

505

516 — TEMPLE — FINISHED

518

THE BOOK OF ZECHARIAH

| 1:1 | 1:7 | 7:1 | 9:1 | 14:21 |

Zechariah begins to preach

Visions are seen

Zechariah continues preaching

PROPHECIES OF END TIMES

Haggai continues to minister

THE BOOK OF HAGGAI

| 1:1 | 1:15 | 2:10 | 2:23 |

Haggai begins to preach

work on Temple begins

Haggai continues preaching

THE PROPHET

23 days

3-4 months

3-4 months

2 months

11-12 months

~ 2 years

4 years

520

49

a. Not all the objects and actions of a vision symbolize something. Decide what the prominent symbols are, and seek interpretations of these which agree with the overall picture of the vision.

b. Use a commentary for help, especially in interpreting unclear symbols (e.g., white horse).

c. Be inquisitive like the prophet ("What are these?"). But do not be impatient if you do not understand all the details of each vision. Even Zechariah did not learn from the angel the meaning of every detail.

d. One of your main tasks will be to determine if a vision was about only the present *and* future.[2] In the Bible *most* apocalyptic visions are about the future, that is, the end times (cf. Rev. 1:19; 4:1-11).

II. ANALYSIS

Passages to be analyzed: 1:1-6; 1:7-6:8; 6:9-15
Paragraph divisions: at verses 1:1, 7, 12, 18; 2:1, 6; 3:1, 6; 4:1; 5:1, 5; 6:1, 9. Mark these in your Bible now.

Since this lesson involves a long section of Zechariah's book, you will want to study it in smaller units for practical purposes. It is better to move slowly than to skim over the surface.

A. The Passage as a Whole

1. Review survey Chart K, observing that this passage is of three main parts: opening paragraph, eight visions, closing paragraph. This is shown below.

1:1	1:7	6:9 6:15
THE WAY OF SALVATION "Turn"	EIGHT NIGHT VISIONS	THE BRINGER OF SALVATION "Branch"

2. If future, it must also be determined if this was near future, or the church age, or the end times. G. Campbell Morgan says, "This series of visions constitutes the Old Testament Apocalypse, or unveiling of *God's Final Dealings with Israel*" (*The Analyzed Bible* [Westwood, N.J.: Revell, 1944], p. 343, italics added).

Chart M

THE EIGHT VISIONS OF ZECHARIAH

	1 / 1:7-17	2 / 1:18-21	3 / 2:1-13	4 / 3:1-10	5 / 4:1-14	6 / 5:1-4	7 / 5:5-11	8 / 6:1-8
identifying titles	Lord's patrol	four horns and carpenters	measuring line	High Priest Joshua	candlestick and olive trees	flying roll	woman in ephah	four chariots
main subject	heathen at ease; blessing awaits Israel	ISRAEL				ALL THE EARTH		
references to Israel	chosen	avenged	multiplied	cleansed	used			
judgment	Gentiles condemned							
references to Temple	1:16			3:7	4:9			
Israel in prophecy	relative rest during restoration	persecution and scattering; then persecutors punished	Israel's prosperity	Israel's sins removed; Christ seen as Messiah	Israel, God's future light-bearer			
THE LORD AND THE WHOLE EARTH	LORD DETERMINES NATIONS' DESTINIES							LORD CONTROLS THE WORLD

51

What common subject is suggested by the opening and closing of paragraphs?

Could this be a clue to a theme of the eight visions?

2. It will be helpful next to make an overall survey of the eight visions. Use the work sheet of Chart M to record observations along the way. (Things to look for are suggested below.) Some observations and outlines already appear on the chart.

3. Read each vision and record, in your own words, the main subject of each (example is given). Observe how often Zechariah asked the question, "What be these?" Was he always given an answer?

4. Scan the visions again, noting which ones make some reference to Israel (e.g., Jerusalem, Judah, Zion). (Note: Only the all-inclusive word "Israel" appears in the outlines shown on Chart M.) Which visions do not make any reference to Israel and have a universal application in mind (e.g., "all the earth")?[3] Compare your conclusions with the outline shown on the chart.

5. Which visions speak of judgment?

6. Which visions specifically mention the Temple? Some expositors see implied references in the other visions.[4] Why is it not surprising that the Temple would appear in Zechariah's visions?

7. In light of what you have learned about visions so far, think of contemporary applications that God intended Zechariah to make of them, involving the Jews living in those days.

8. Now think of the visions as predicting far-distant events. Study the outline of Chart M, "Israel in Prophecy."[5] Does each application fairly represent the respective vision? Do you see a general chronological progression in the outline? If so, what vision awaits fulfillment next in Israel's time-table? How should Christians today respond to such prophecies about Israel? The classic New Testament passage that teaches that Israel will play an important role in the end times in Romans 11.

9. Compare the first and last visions. How are they compared on the chart? What does this tell you about prophecy and about the Lord?

---

3. The reference to Shinar (Babylon) in 5:11 does not single out Israel by way of contrast, even though Babylon had been Israel's major foe. In Zechariah's time, Babylon was a symbol of the seat of universal wickedness and idolatry. And it is not mere coincidence that Babylon is the last wicked city described in the Bible (Rev. 18).

4. See George L. Robinson, "Book of Zechariah," in *The International Standard Bible Encyclopedia,* 5:3137.

5. Adapted from Henrietta Mears, *What the Bible Is All About,* pp. 330-31.

B. Paragraph by Paragraph

Now focus your attention on the smaller details of each of the paragraphs of this lesson. The questions and study suggestions given below are not exhaustive. Let them be starters of analysis in the paragraphs.

1. *The Way of Salvation: 1:1-6*
Read the paragraph. What is the key command of the Lord?

_____

Compare the two phrases: "Turn ye unto me" and "I will turn unto you."
How does the *combined* truth teach you how a person is saved?

_____

Compare this combination with that of Ephesians 2:8-9.
What were the people to turn from?

_____

Compare 1:5 with Isaiah 40:6-8.

_____

_____

2. *First Vision, The Lord's Patrol: 1:7-17*
Compare "all the earth sitteth still, and is at rest" (1:11) with "the heathen [Gentiles] that are at ease" (1:15).
What must the prophecies of 1:16-17 have meant to Zechariah and his Jewish brethren?

_____

3. *Second Vision, Four Horns and Four Craftsmen: 1:18-21*
See *Notes* on "horns." Did the four horns symbolize something that had already happened? If so, how would this bolster the surety of fulfillment of the four craftsmen ("carpenters," KJV)?

_____

_____

Do you think this vision may have encouraged the people to keep working on the Temple building? Recall from your previous studies who had been the main source of harassment.

4. *Third Vision, Measuring Line: 2:1-13*
Read 2:1-5. What does verse 4 teach?

_____

_____

Verse 5?

Have these prophecies been fulfilled yet? If not, when will they be fulfilled? Recall Chart I.

Read the lyrical poem of 2:6-13. What is the main theme?

Does it expand the descriptions of 2:4-5?
Note how Gentile nations will be influenced by Israel's future ministry (2:11). Did the message of salvation first come to the Gentiles via Israel? Read Romans 11:11-15.

5. *Fourth Vision, High Priest Joshua: 3:1-10*
Read the entire chapter, underlining key words and phrases as you read. Did these strike you: Joshua, the high priest, Satan, filthy garments, iniquity, my house, my servant the Branch?
Begin your analysis of this vision with Israel's problem: "the iniquity of that land" (3:9). Conclude with the divine, atoning work, "I will remove the iniquity" (3:9). According to the vision, how does the change come about?

Apply this to both Israel and to all sinners. Who is "the Branch"? (Cf. Isa. 4:2; 11:1; Jer. 23:5-7; 33:15.)
Note the phrase "behold the stone" (3:9). One writer comments, "The immediate reference is probably to the head-stone of the temple; but the ultimate reference is to Christ, the 'chief corner stone' of the spiritual house."[6] Read 1 Peter 2:6-8.

6. *Fifth Vision, Candlestick and Olive Trees: 4:1-14*
Read the paragraph, underlining key words and phrases as you read.
How many lamps were on the candlestick (lampstand) (4:2)?

In verse 10 the Lord through the angel told Zechariah what the lamps symbolized: "Do not despise this small beginning, for the eyes of the Lord rejoice to see the work begin, to see the plumb-line in the hand of Zerubbabel. For these seven lamps represent the eyes of the Lord that see everywhere around the world" (*The Living Bible*). The bowl of the lampstand (4:2) was fed continuous-

---

6. G. Collins, "Zechariah, " in *The New Bible Commentary*, p. 751.

ly with oil from the two olive trees (4:12). What did the two olive trees and branches symbolize (4:14)?

_____

_____

The "two anointed ones" are generally interpreted as being the Lord's two servants, the governor, Zerubbabel, and the high priest, Joshua.
The main thrust of this vision appears in verses 6-10. What things are taught here about the Temple?

_____

_____

In this context, what is the impact of the oft-quoted words "Not by might, nor by power, but by my spirit" (4:6)?

_____

_____

If the Temple was a symbol of Israel's worship of God, was it a witness to the whole world of this truth? Observe in the vision that twice the Lord is identified with "the whole earth." May this suggest a worldwide ministry of saved Israel?
7. *Sixth Vision, Flying Roll: 5:1-4*
Read the paragraph. The word "roll" means "scroll." Can you visualize the size of the scroll? (One cubit equals one and a half feet.) What is the main teaching of this vision?

_____

_____

How widespread is the judgment?

_____

Relate the plight symbolized in this vision to the solution symbolized in the preceding vision.

_____

_____

8. *Seventh Vision, Woman in Ephah: 5:5-11*
Read the paragraph. List the main objects and actions of this vision. (Don't press small details in a vision.) Are any interpreted?

Try arriving at your own interpretations of the other symbols. How do you interpret the removal of the ephah[7] bearing the woman?

_____

_____

What would such a vision say to Israelites who had just returned from exile in Babylon (Shinar)?

_____

_____

9. Eighth Vision, Four Chariots: 6:1-8

Read the paragraph. In those days what were chariots usually used for?

_____

Does this suggest what the chariots symbolize?

_____

What is the function of the chariots in the vision? (See *Notes* on "north country," 6:8.)

_____

How is this vision related to the two preceding ones, as far as judgment is concerned?

_____

Who is the supreme judge over all the world, according to this vision?

_____

10. The Bringer of Salvation: 6:9-15

The vision of four chariots (6:1-8) was the last of the eight visions seen by Zechariah. When they were over, the Lord had some important instructions for the prophet. He was about to write one of the most comprehensive yet compact messianic prophecies in the Old Testament.

Read 6:9-15, and try to visualize the action as you read. Observe this sequence:

    a. Offering of the exiles (6:10)
    b. Crown[8] made and placed on Joshua the high priest (6:11)
    c. Messianic teaching (6:12-13)
    d. Memorial to the donors (6:14)

_____

7. An ephah was a large bushel basket.
8. See Notes.

What does the first half of verse 15 add to what the Lord had instructed Zechariah?

_____

Analyze the messianic message of 6:12-13. What are your thoughts about the following phrases, as applied to Christ:

"Behold the man"
"The Branch . . . shall [branch out] grow up."
"He shall build the temple" (cf. 1 Pet. 2:5).
"He shall bear the glory."
"He shall sit and rule upon his throne."
"He shall be a priest."
"The counsel of peace shall be between them both."⁹

III. NOTES

1. *"Myrtle trees"* (1:8). In the Bible myrtle trees often symbolized Israel.
2. *"The earth . . . is at rest"* (1:11). Feinberg comments, "Actually, the early years of Darius' reign had been stormy, marked by repeated rebellions throughout his domain; but in this year all was calm again."¹⁰
3. *"Four horns"* (1:18). Horns symbolized power. The number four often represented the four quarters of the earth.
4. *"Fair mitre"* (3:5). This was a clean turban. Kings wore crowns; priests wore turbans.
5. *"Protested unto"* (3:6). It also has been translated as "admonished" (NASB).
6. *"Judge my house"* (3:7). The meaning is "govern my house."
7. *"Headstone"* (4:7). Placing the headstone on the Temple building marked the completion to the project.
8. *"House of the thief, and . . . house of him that sweareth falsely"* (5:4). The Bible often cites parts of the Ten Commandments to represent the whole (cf. James 2:10). Feinberg suggests a reason why these two sins were cited here:

> Stealing was a violation of the middle commandment of the second table of the law; swearing falsely by God's name transgressed the middle commandment of the first table. Men who violated these commandments were false to God and man.¹¹

9. That is, between the offices of priest and king (cf. Heb. 5:10; 7:1; Ps. 110:4).
10. *The Wycliffe Bible Commentary*, p. 899.
11. *The Wycliffe Bible Commentary*, p. 902.

9. *"Talents of lead"* (5:7). This was a heavy lead cover on the bushel basket.

10. *"North country . . . south country"* (6:6). Because chariots are in this vision, military might seems to be involved. With relation to the land of Israel, Babylon was the enemy of the north. (Babylonian invaders came upon Israel from the north, avoiding the impassable desert that lay between Canaan and Babylon.) Egypt was the formidable power to the south.

11. *"Crowns"* (6:11). "The original indicates one splendid crown made up of several circlets."[12]

12. *"They that are far off"* (6:15). The deputation from Babylon represents Gentiles who will come from all over the world in the reign of the Messiah to help build the Lord's Temple (cf. Isa. 60:10-11).

13. *"The Lord your God"* (6:15). This is the only appearance of the name God (Heb., *Elohim*, God as the Creator) in chapters 1-6.

IV. FOR THOUGHT AND DISCUSSION

1. What is repentance? What is conversion?

2. Was Israel intended to be God's channel of revelation to Gentiles in Old Testament days? If so, how successful was the mission? What will be the relationship between the two peoples in the end times (2:11)? Compare Psalm 67; Isaiah 2:3; 60:3.

3. What does 3:1 teach about Satan?

4. What are the ministries of Christ as the believer's High Priest? Hebrews says much about this. Also see John 17.)

5. How is the humility of Christ represented by the two titles "servant" and "branch"? Why was Christ manifested in this way?

6. Why does God use human instruments to accomplish His crucial work on earth? (Cf. 4:14.)

7. What are your reflections about this truth: "Not by might, nor by power, but by my spirit, saith the Lord of hosts" (4:6)?

8. What attributes of God are prominent in chapters 1-6?

9. In what sense is the stage being set in Palestine today for events foreshadowed in Zechariah?

V. FURTHER STUDY

1. With the help of an exhaustive concordance, see how often the words "temple" and God's "house" appear in Zechariah.

---

12. Ibid., p.903.

2. Study the appearances of the names "God" and "Lord" in the three postexilic prophets. The name Lord ("Jehovah") has the meaning of Saviour.

3. You may want to make an extended study of the many symbols of Zechariah's visions. Refer to commentaries.

VI. WORDS TO PONDER

CHRIST'S FIRST ADVENT

I bring you the most joyful news ever announced, and it is for everyone! The Savior—yes, the Messiah, the Lord—has been born tonight in Bethlehem! (Luke 2:10-11, *The Living Bible*).

CHRIST'S SECOND ADVENT

Be silent, all mankind, before the Lord, for he has come to earth from heaven, from his holy home (Zech. 2:13, *The Living Bible*).

What About Fasting?

This lesson is about four messages that the Lord gave Zechariah to deliver to His people. Actually the messages were God's answers to one question about fasting, which a delegation from Bethel had asked.

Some very important spiritual lessons about a believer's relationship to God can be learned from the passage of this lesson. Think of it. Fasting in the book of Zechariah has much to say to you 2,500 years later. That is how contemporary the Bible is.

I. PREPARATION FOR STUDY

1. Review survey Chart K. Observe how chapters 7-8 are identified in the outlines. How much time had transpired since Zechariah had seen the night visions?

2. Read Zechariah 8:19. Note that the people were keeping fasts in these months: fourth, fifth, seventh, and tenth. Now read 2 Kings 25, which records the original events memorialized by those fasts. The occasion was the fall of Jerusalem in 586 B.C. Note the following in the 2 Kings passage:

Tenth month (ninth year)—siege of Jerusalem began (25:1).
Fourth month (eleventh year)—city was taken (25:3-4).
Fifth month (eleventh year)—city was burned (25:8-9).
Seventh month (eleventh year)—Gedaliah was slain (25:25).

3. Since the Jews had now returned to the city that was the object of destruction recorded in 2 Kings 25, do you think it was natural that they would have a question about whether they should keep on observing the fasts? (Note: Originally the fasts were evidently self-imposed ones, since there is no record in the Bible of a divine command to observe them.)

II. ANALYSIS

Segments to be analyzed: 7:1-7; 7:8-14; 8:1-17; 8:18-23
Paragraph divisions: at verses 7:1, 8; 8:1, 9, 14, 18. (Mark these in your Bible.)

A. The Passage as a Whole

If you did not do so in the survey study of Lesson 5, underline in your Bible the phrase "the word of the Lord came" at these verses: 7:1, 8; 8:1,18. The four messages to Zechariah begin at these four points; mark these beginnings clearly in your Bible.

B. Segment by Segment

1. *The People's Question and the Lord's First Answer: 7:1-7*
Read 7:1-3. (See *Notes* on the phrase "house of God," 7:2.) What was the delegates' question, and what were they implying?[1]

_____

_____

In your own words, interpret what the Lord meant by each of these three replies:
7:5

_____

7:6

_____

7:7

_____

Compare the readings of a modern paraphrase (e.g., *The Living Bible*).

2. *Second Answer: 7:8-14*
Read the entire paragraph. This second reply is of three parts:
   7:9-10, how the *fasting* Israelites should be *living*
   7:11-12, why the fall of Jerusalem came in the first place
   7:13-14, the principle of just recompense, with the key word, "therefore"

---

1. Only one fast—that of the fifth month—is reported in 7:3. But compare 7:5 and 8:19.

In your own words, what was the Lord telling His people here?

_____

_____

3. *Third Answer: 8:1-17*

Many regard Zechariah 8 as one of the most beautiful chapters in the entire Old Testament. What makes this all the more significant is that the words arise out of the crucible of judgment and mourning. Read 8:1-8. What things does the Lord promise to do?

_____

_____

Have any of these been fulfilled? Would you say that the descriptions apply more to the messianic Kingdom of the end times?

_____

Read 8:9-13. What verses definitely applied to Zechariah's time?

_____

Note the appeal of verse 9 concerning the Temple. Have verses 12 and 13 been fulfilled yet?

_____

Read 8:14-17. Here are recorded the conditions for Israel's blessing. What are those conditions?

_____

_____

How was this third answer like the second (7:9-10)?

_____

_____

In your own words, what was the Lord trying to tell the people here that would make them reflect more about their question of fasting?

_____

_____

4. *Fourth Answer: 8:18-23*

Read 8:18-19. What beautiful truth about true fasting is taught here?

_____

How had this been illustrated in the Lord's third answer (8:1-17)?

_____

Read 8:20-23. What is the prominent prophecy in these verses?

_____

Why should such a promise rejoice the heart of believing Israel?

_____

Note the last phrase, "God is with you" (8:23). One of the Lord's names is Immanuel (Isa. 7:14), which means literally "God with us."

III. NOTES

1. "House of God" (7:2). The Hebrew is *Beth-el* ("house of God"). Most modern versions translate the word to refer to the city of Bethel. "Now the town of Bethel had sent Sharezer" (NASB).
2. "Jealous for her with great fury" (8:2). The Berkeley Version reads, "With glowing jealousy I am burning for her." The picture is one of intense love and protection of Israel by the Lord.
3. "Many people and strong nations shall come to seek the Lord" (8:22). Of this wonderful climax of the Temple's ministries, Calvin writes:

> The temple was built for this end and purpose—that the doctrine of salvation might continue there, and have its seat there until the coming of Christ; for then was fulfilled that prophecy in the hundred and tenth Psalm, "The sceptre of Thy power shall God send forth from Sion." The Prophet here teaches us that Christ would not be the king of one people only . . . but that He would rule through the whole world.[2]

IV. FOR THOUGHT AND DISCUSSION

1. If you are studying in a group, you will want to spend much time discussing the important subject of fasting. Suggestions for discussion are given below.
a. What is your definition of fasting?
b. Mourning and praying are often associated with fasting in the Bible (Zech. 7:5; Acts 13:3). Why?
c. Some examples of fasting in the New Testament are by Jesus (Matt. 4:2) and the Christians at Antioch (Acts 13:2-3). Actually,

_____

2. F. Davidson, ed., *The New Bible Commentary,* p. 755.

there are relatively few references to Christians fasting in the New Testament.[3] Why do you suppose this is so?

d. What should be a person's genuine motive in fasting? Read Isaiah 58:1-12, and you will see the kinds of motives in fasting that God rejects.

e. A good measure of a person's heart in fasting is how he acts in days of feasting (Zech. 7:6). Why?

2. Many people do not believe there will be a literal millennial kingdom on earth mainly because it is difficult for them to visualize the fulfillment of the prophecies. Note what the Lord said to His people, "This seems unbelievable to you ... but it is no great thing for me" (Zech. 8:6, *The Living Bible*).

3. The Lord saw the Jews' successful witness to Gentiles as a cause for deep joy (8:19-23). Why is personal witnessing by a Christian such a joyous experience?

4. What have you learned from Zechariah 7-8 that will help you to be a better Christian?

V. FURTHER STUDY

1. Go through Zechariah 7-8, and note every command. What are your conclusions?

2. You may want to read extended works on the subject of fasting.

3. Read G. Campbell Morgan, *Voices of Twelve Hebrew Prophets*,[4] chapter 11, for an interesting essay on Zechariah 8:5 (boys and girls playing in the streets).

VI. WORDS TO PONDER

The Lord of Hosts says, Get on with the job and finish it! You have been listening long enough! (Zech. 8:9, *The Living Bible*).

---

3. This is especially so in the epistles, where we might expect such exhortations. Paul's references in 2 Cor. 6:5 and 11:27 are apparently about involuntary fastings.
4. G. Campbell Morgan, *Voices of Twelve Hebrew Prophets* (London: Pickering & Inglis, n.d.).

Israel's History to the End of Time

Chapters 9-11 of Zechariah prophesy major events of Israel's history up to the end times. The passage is introduced as a "burden" (9:1), a common word in the prophetic books, meaning an ominous oracle of judgments to come. But the three chapters are not only about judgment, as we shall see.

I. PREPARATION FOR STUDY

1. It was probably some time after the Temple project was finished that Zechariah was inspired of God to write the remainder of his book (chaps. 9-14). The style of this later writing is different from that of the earlier chapters, partly because much of the subject matter is different.[1]

2. The passage of this lesson is admittedly one of the most difficult of all the prophetic books to interpret. Suggestions for study given in this lesson are intended to alleviate the difficult interpretations. Do not be frustrated if you do not understand every part of the Bible passage. Let this be a challenge for further study at a later time. Major on the highlights and broad movements of the Bible text, which will provide much spiritual food for thought.

3. Before studying the passage, it will help to have clearly in mind a general pattern of Israel's history from the time of Zechariah to the end times. Chart N shows the highlights of that history.[2]

An important part of your Bible study will be to decide what aspect (event or era) of Israel's history Zechariah is prophesying about in each paragraph.

---

1. The unity of the book, with one author, is not jeopardized by this change of style.
2. The phrases "first advent" and "second advent" refer to Jesus' comings to the earth.

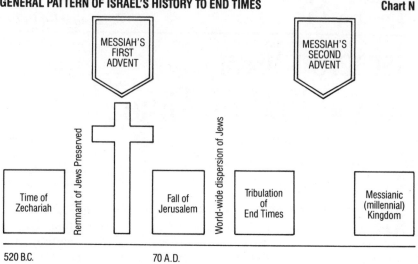

II. ANALYSIS

Segments to be analyzed: 9:1-17; 10:1-12; 11:1-17
Paragraph divisions[3]: at verses 9:1, 9, 10; 10:1, 3, 5, 8; 11:1, 4, 15.
(Mark these in your Bible.)

A. The Passages as a Whole

1. The work sheet of Chart O is built around the chronological sequence shown on Chart N (sequence advances from left to right). Use Chart O to record where you think each paragraph of the three chapters should be located timewise. For example, the paragraph of 9:9 is identified on the chart under *first advent*, since this prophecy of Jesus' entry into Jerusalem was clearly fulfilled at that time. (Read Matt. 21:1-11 after you have read Zech. 9:9.)

Read the other paragraphs of Zechariah 9-11, and try to place each one at the appropriate place on Chart O. A suggested set of locations appears on Chart P, but you should not feel restricted to accept that arrangement.

2. Chart P shows possible identifications of the prophecies of the ten paragraphs of Zechariah 9-11. Approach the paragraphs

---

3. Sometimes in this passage a new paragraph division is hard to detect. This contributes to the difficulty of interpreting some of the prophecies, as to when they should be fulfilled. The interpretations of this lesson are based on this set of paragraph divisions.

66

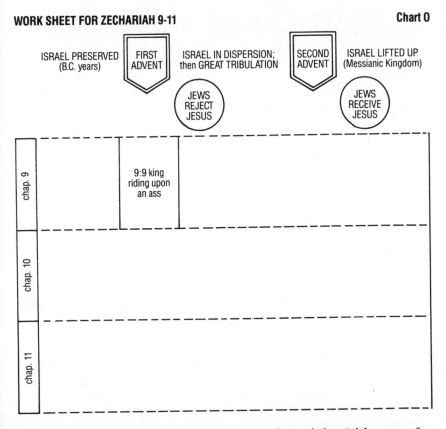

one by one, doing these three things: (1) read the Bible text of each paragraph; (2) see where the paragraph is located on the chart; (3) read the reasons given for interpreting the text that way.

9:1-8. Note that many Gentile cites are mentioned in the text. Most expositors see this prophecy fulfilled in the conquests of Alexander the Great in the fourth century B.C.[4] Observe that Israel was to be protected (9:8). This paragraph is thus identified on Chart P with the B.C. years leading up to Christ's first advent.

9:9. This was discussed earlier in the lesson.

9:10-17. Among the prominent pictures in this paragraph are peace (v. 10); victory of Jews over Gentiles (vv. 13-15); reigning of Israel (v. 16). These are pictures of the messianic Kingdom. (How long a time, then, separates 9:9 and 9:10?)

---

4. See *The Wycliffe Bible Commentary,* pp. 905-6; and *The New Bible Commentary,* pp. 755-56.

10:1-2. Verse 2 is the key. It is a picture of false diviners and "no shepherd." The people (Jews) are thus a troubled flock. In view of the paragraphs that follow, 10:1-2 may be describing Israel in dispersion throughout the world, between the two advents of Christ.

10:3-4. Verse 3 speaks of the Lord's deliverance of Judah from false shepherds. This is the battle setting for His second advent, described figuratively by verse 4: "From them will come the Cornerstone, the Peg on which all hope hangs, the Bow that wins the battle, the Ruler over all the earth" (*The Living Bible*). Feinberg comments on this verse:

> From Judah specifically, just mentioned in verse 3, will come forth King Messiah. The figures used represent the Messiah in his strength, stability, and trustworthiness. Compare Isa. 19:13 (ASV); 1 Pet. 2:6; Isa. 22:23, 24; Ex. 15:3; Ps. 45:4,5.[5]

So this paragraph is identified on Chart P with the Lord's second advent.

10:5-7. Verse 5 refers to the battle of 10:3, and verses 6-7 describe the blessings that will come to Israel in their triumph.

10:8-12. This is a more extended description of Israel's restoration in the messianic Kingdom. The four paragraphs of chapter 10 thus give an uninterrupted panorama of the Jews' history from their rejection of Jesus to their worship of Him in the Millennium.

11:1-3. Chapter 11 reverts back to Israel's woes before Christ's second advent. This first paragraph figuratively introduces the theme of judgment.

11:4-14. Many parts of this long paragraph are difficult to understand. Read 11:12-13. This prophecy was fulfilled when Judas betrayed Jesus. (Read Matt. 26:14-16; 27:3-10.)[6] When this clue is pursued, the paragraph is seen to be about the *Good Shepherd Rejected.* (Refer to a commentary for interpretation of the various parts of the paragraph.)

11:15-17. This paragraph is about a false shepherd. Feinberg comments:

> They rejected the true Shepherd; they must have the rule of the false or foolish shepherd. Morally, this is any one of the many wicked rulers who have plagued Israel through the centuries.

---

5. *The Wycliffe Bible Commentary*, p. 907.
6. See Hobart E. Freeman, *An Introduction to the Old Testament Prophets*, pp. 340-42, for a discussion of the problem arising out of Matthew's reference to Jeremiah in Matt. 27:9.

| | ISRAEL PRESERVED (B.C. years) | FIRST ADVENT | ISRAEL IN DISPERSION; then GREAT TRIBULATION | SECOND ADVENT | ISRAEL LIFTED UP (Messianic Kingdom) |

JEWS REJECT JESUS

JEWS RECEIVE JESUS

chap. 9

| 9:1 | 9:9 | | 9:10 | 9:17 |
| GENTILE CITIES FALL (Israel protected) | KING JESUS COMES | | ISRAEL IN TRIUMPH AND GLORY | |

chap. 10

| 10:1 | 10:3 | 10:5 | 10:8-12 |
| WANDERING SHEEP | MESSIAH COMES FORTH | ISRAEL TRIUMPHS OVER FOES | FULL RESTOR-ATION |

chap. 11

| 11:1 | 11:4 | 11:15-17 |
| Theme of Judgment | GOOD SHEPHERD REJECTED | BAD SHEPHERD ACCEPTED |

The culmination will appear in the counterfeit of Christ who will arise at the end-time. (See Dan. 11:36-39; 2 Thess. 2:1-12; Rev. 13:11-18).[7]

So the paragraph is located just before Christ's second advent.

B. Paragraph Study

Now that you have viewed the three chapters in a general way, return to each individual paragraph and study some of the details on your own. Look for the kinds of things mentioned in earlier lessons under the heading *Paragraph by Paragraph*. Refer to commentaries for help in interpreting the many symbols and figures of speech.

7. *The Wycliffe Bible Commentary*, p. 908.

III. NOTES

1. *"In the land of Hadrach"* (9:1). Read 9:1-2 in *The Living Bible* for a clear paraphrase of what is intended by the two verses.

2. *"No oppressor shall pass through them [Israelites] any more"* (9:8). A strict fulfillment of this will come only in the end times. If the verses preceding this are about Alexander's conquests, then the prophet is leaping over the centuries to prophesy a *climactic* deliverance. This prophetical law of extension is used from time to time in the Bible.[8]

3. *"Thy sons, O Zion, against thy sons, O Greece"* (9:13). Some interpret this as a prophecy of Jewish military victories in the Maccabean wars (175-163 B.C.). If it is a multiple prophecy, it also may refer to Israel's victories over their enemies in the end times. This was the basis for placing 9:10-17 on Chart P as yet to be fulfilled.

4. *"They went their own way as a flock"* (10:2). "They wander like sheep" (NASB), is an apt description of Jews in the Dispersion.

IV. FOR THOUGHT AND DISCUSSION

1. What have you learned about the mercy of the Lord from your studies in this lesson?

2. If you are studying with a group, you may want to discuss the role of Israel in world history now and in the years to come.

V. FURTHER STUDY

1. Spend more time studying 11:4-17 with the help of commentaries.

2. False shepherds and good shepherds appear throughout the Bible. You may want to pursue this subject.

VI. WORDS TO PONDER

Rejoice greatly, O my people! Shout with joy! For look—your King is coming! (Zech. 9:9, *The Living Bible*).

---

8. Another interpretation of 9:1-8 is that the whole paragraph is about the end times.

Lesson 9

King over All

Zechariah's prophecies climax in the last three chapters about the Lord as King over all. The brightest hopes of Israel concern the last days, when God will deliver the nation from all oppressors and bring it into His Son's Kingdom. That day of salvation will come only when the people finally repent of their sins (12:10) and acknowledge the crucified Jesus as their Messiah.

I. PREPARATION FOR STUDY

1. Review the survey Chart K, and try to recall the highlights of all the previous lessons.

2. Review Chart N, which shows the general pattern of Israel's history up to the time of the Millennium. The following events or eras of this chart will appear in the Bible passage of this lesson:

 a. Christ's first advent to this earth
 b. World-wide dispersion of the Jews
 c. Tribulation of end-times
 d. Christ's second advent to this earth
 e. The millennial Kingdom

Concerning the Tribulation period, it should be noted here that the Jews will experience their worst trials at this time. Then at the end of the period many Jews will be converted and turn to Christ (Zech. 12:10–13:3; Ezek. 36:24-29; 37:1-14; Rom. 11:25-26). It is at this time that Christ will come to the earth (second advent) and slay all the armies fighting against Israel in the Battle of Armageddon. (Read Rev. 19:11-21.) That battle ushers in the millennial Kingdom (Rev. 20:1-6).

II. ANALYSIS

Segments to be analyzed: 12:1-14; 13:1-9; 14:1-21
Paragraph divisions: at verses 12:1, 10; 13:1, 7; 14:1, 6, 12, 16

A. The Segment as a Whole

Chart Q outlines the content of chapters 12-14. Spend time with the chart to become acquainted with the overall contents of the passage.

1. Read 12:1–14:21 paragraph by paragraph, noting as you read how each paragraph is represented by a title on the chart (e.g., Israel's deliverance). You may want to assign your own titles.

2. Next, observe on the chart how the passage is divided into three main parts. Then note the two-part outline: The People; The King. In chapters 12-13, the action is mainly about the people of Israel (even though the smitten Christ is the key to the people's fortunes). In chapter 14 the spotlight is on the King, Jesus.

SURVEY OF ZECHARIAH 12–14   Chart Q

CONSUMMATION OF ISRAEL'S HISTORY							
12:1	12:10	13:1	13:7	14:1	14:6	14:12	14:16-21
Israel's Deliverance	Israel's Mourning	Israel's Cleansing by Water	Israel's Refining by Fire; Glorification	Advent of Messiah	King over All	Enemies Punished	Holiness unto the Lord
ISRAEL'S DELIVERANCE		ISRAEL'S CLEANSING		ISRAEL WORSHIPS			
The People				The King			
CHRIST'S CROSS (12:10; 13:7)				CHRIST'S CROWN (14:9)			

3. There are two key prophecies of Christ's death in 12:1–13:9. Read 12:10 and 13:7. Then read John 19:37 and Matthew 26:31, which quote the prophecies at the time of their fulfillment.

4. There is a progression in the four paragraphs of 12:1–13:9. Follow it in the descriptions below.

a. *Israel's Deliverance.* This will take place in the last days (note the repetition "in that day").

b. *Israel's Mourning.* Out of the military deliverance of 12:1-9 will come a spiritual awakening (12:10). Jews will mourn over Christ, whom they had rejected.

c. *Israel's Cleansing.* The contrite heart of 12:10-14 will bring the spiritual cleansing of 13:1.

d. *Israel's Refining and Glorification.* The spiritual awakening of 13:1 will bring Israel's final glorification (13:9*b*). Before Zechariah writes of that experience, however, he describes a panoramic vision of Israel from the time of Christ's death ("smite the shepherd") to the years of the Tribulation. Compare the fountain cleansing of 13:1 with the fire refining (13:9*a*).

5. Chapter 14 shows Christ as king and lord over all. What pictures of Christ as king do you see in the four paragraphs of chapter 14?

6. Note how often the name *Jerusalem* appears in chapter 14. Why is this?

B. Paragraph by Paragraph

There is much to learn from analyzing these paragraphs. Let the few study suggestions given below be starters for your analysis. Recall from earlier in the lesson what has already been observed concerning each paragraph.

1. *Israel's Deliverance: 12:1-9*
Note the many references to "all the people." Who are they? What point is made consistently?

_____

_____

How does 12:9 summarize the paragraph?

_____

_____

2. *Israel's Mourning: 12:10-14*
What do you think is meant by "the spirit of grace and supplications" (12:10)?

_____

_____

73

Who originates this spiritual endowment? Compare Ezekiel 39:25-29; Joel 2:28-29.

What is the repeated word of verses 10-11?

3. *Israel's Cleansing: 13:1-6*
Compare 13:1 with Ezekiel 36:24-27. Is the "fountain . . . for sin and uncleanness" a literal fountain? If not, what is it? Compare John 19:34.

4. *Israel's Glorification: 13:7-9*
Do you see the humanity and deity of Jesus in the "the man that is my fellow" (13:7)?
What different truths are taught by the two statements of 13:9:
"It is my people"
"The Lord is my God"
5. *Key Phrases: Chapter 14*
Below are listed key phrases of this concluding chapter of Zechariah. What spiritual truths do they teach you?
  14:1 —"The day of the Lord cometh."
  14:4 —"His feet shall stand . . . upon the mount of Olives."
  14:5 —"The Lord my God shall come, and all the saints with Him."[1]
  14:8 —"Living waters shall go out from Jerusalem."
  14:9 —"The Lord shall be King over all the earth."
  14:9 —"There shall be one Lord."
  14:11—"No more utter destruction."
  14:20—"HOLINESS UNTO THE LORD."
  14:21—"No more the Canaanite in the house of the Lord of hosts."

III. FOR THOUGHT AND DISCUSSION

1. Recall the two references to Christ's death in the passage of this lesson. Why is the death of Christ the key to Israel's salvation? Why does Israel today reject Christ's blood atonement?

1. NASB translates the last word as "Him" rather than "thee," on the basis of ancient versions.

2. What is your definition of grace? Consider the different things that are suggested by this statement: "Grace is everything for nothing to the sinner who doesn't deserve anything" (Lehman Strauss).

3. These last three chapters of Zechariah are specific prophecies about Israel. But the applications need not to be confined to Israel. Go through the three chapters once again, and list the spiritual truths that may be applied to Christians and nonsaved. If you are studying with a group, compare your findings with the other members.

A CONCLUDING THOUGHT

In that day . . . the trash cans in the Temple of the Lord will be as sacred as the bowls beside the altar (Zech. 14:20, *The Living Bible*).

Lesson 10
Background and Survey of Malachi

The book of Malachi contains the Lord's last recorded words of Old Testament times. In many respects it is a sad book because it reveals what little progress—if any—Israel had made since the nation was born 1,500 years earlier (Gen. 12). Dark and distressing as the book is, however, the sun of God's grace arises out of its pages, so that when the reader has arrived at the last verse there is no question but that in the end the day of glory will come for a repentant Israel, as well as for all believers.

I. BACKGROUND OF THE BOOK

A. The Man Malachi

The Bible furnishes no biographical information about Malachi. He was a prophet of God (1:1), a contemporary of Nehemiah. His name is an abbreviated form of the Hebrew *Malachiah*, which means "messenger of Jehovah." It is interesting that the word "messenger" appears three times in this short book. (Read 2:7 and 3:1.)

B. The Book of Malachi

1. *Date*. Malachi probably wrote his book around the time of Nehemiah's visit to Babylon in 433 B.C. (Neh. 13:6). See Chart D. In support of this view are these facts:

a. The Temple project had already been completed, and Mosaic sacrifices were being offered (Mal. 1:7-10; 3:1, 8). See Chart D for the date when the Temple was completed.

b. A Persian governor, not Nehemiah, was ruling the Jews at the time. Read 1:8.[1]

c. The sins denounced by Malachi were the same sins that Nehemiah dealt with during his second term.[2] For example:

Laxity and corruption of priests (Mal. 1:6–2:9; Neh. 13:1-9)

Mixed marriages (Mal. 2:10-16; Neh. 13:23-28)

Neglect of tithes (Mal. 3:7-12; Neh. 13:10-13)

In the words of G. Campbell Morgan, "the failures of the people that angered Nehemiah, inspired the message of Malachi."[3] Since Nehemiah and Malachi were contemporaries, it would be enlightening to study their two books together.

2. *Occasion and Message.* When Malachi wrote his book, the Jews as a nation had been back in the land of Canaan for about 100 years. Prophets like Haggai and Zechariah had predicted that God's blessings would be given to the people in days to come, especially in "the day of the Lord." " But several decades had passed and these prophecies of hope were still unfulfilled. The days had become increasingly drab and dreary. It was a period of disappointment, disillusionment, and discouragement, of blasted hopes and broken hearts."[4] The Jews' faith and worship were eroding, and their daily lives showed it. In this backslidden condition they were hyper-critical of God's ways. That God would even speak with them is evidence of His long-suffering and mercy.

The main subjects of Malachi's message were the love of God, the sin of the priests and people, judgment for sin, and blessing for righteousness. One cannot help but observe that the gospel of God has been the same message for sinners for all generations.

3. *Features.* The most notable feature of this book is its repeated pattern of discourse.[5] Three steps are involved (example is shown):

AFFIRMATION (charge or accusation): "Ye have robbed me" (3:8).

INTERROGATION (introduced by "ye say"): "But ye say, Wherein have we robbed thee?" (3:8).

---

1. The word *pehah*, translated "governor" in 1:8, is a borrowed word, used for the Persian governors in Palestine in postexilic times. See the *Zondervan Pictorial Bible Dictionary*, p. 503.
2. The revival fires of Nehemiah's earlier ministry (Neh. 10:28-39) had by now died out.
3. G. Campbell Morgan, *Voices of Twelve Hebrew Prophets,* p. 151. Another writer has commented, "The Book of Malachi fits the situation amid which Nehemiah worked as snugly as a bone fits its socket" (J. M. P. Smith, quoted in *The International Standard Bible Encyclopedia,* 3:1970).
4. Ralph Earle, *Meet the Minor Prophets,* p. 105.
5. This pattern has been called didactic-dialectic, or dialogistic.

REFUTATION (answer to the question): "In tithes and offerings" (3:8).

The common repeated phrase in these discourses is "ye say." It appears eight times: 1:2, 6, 7; 2:14, 17; 3:7, 8, 13.

Another feature of Malachi's message is his strong emphasis on the law of God. Read 4:4. Also, the book surpasses all other prophetic books in the proportion of verses spoken by the Lord to Israel (47 out of the total of 55).

4. *The Place of Malachi in the Bible Canon.* Malachi is both a conclusion and a connecting link. It concludes the story of Israel for the span of 2000-400 B.C., and it is the last prophetic voice of the Old Testament. The book connects the Old Testament with New by its prophecies of John the Baptist and Christ's first advent. Its "messianic flashes (3:1-6; 4:2) prepare us for the NT revelation and focus our attention on Him who alone is the world's hope."[6] Beyond that, the book reaches into the end times when it prophesies about the final Day of the Lord (second advent).

II. SURVEY OF THE BOOK

Chart R is a survey chart showing the general pattern and highlights of Malachi. Study it carefully after you have scanned the text of the whole book.

Note the following on the chart. (Read the references in the Bible.)

1. The first verse (1:1) is a typical introduction to the book.

2. The last paragraph (4:4-6) is not only a conclusion to the book but also a fitting conclusion to the whole Old Testament.

3. The first half of the book (1:2–3:15) is mainly about sin. What subjects does Malachi write about after 3:16?

4. What bright prophecy appears at 3:1-6? Why do you think it is spoken in the middle of the section about the people's sins?

5. How does the chart compare the beginning and end of Malachi's prophecy?

6. Note the key words and key verse.

III. APPLYING MALACHI TODAY

The practical teachings of Malachi are numerous. In addition to the messianic prophecies of Kingdom and judgment, the commands about everyday living are timeless. W. Graham Scroggie comments:

6. Merrill F. Unger, *Unger's Bible Handbook,* p. 449.

MALACHI WILL A MAN ROB GOD?

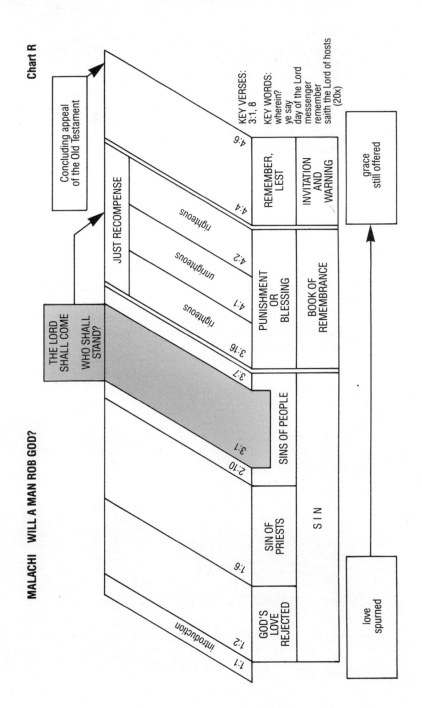

Chart R

Malachi's message is eminently necessary and appropriate today, for these abuses have their equivalents in the modern Church. How prevalent is "a form of godliness," the power being denied; how weak are multitudes of Christians with regard to great moral questions; how frequent is alliance in marriage of saved and unsaved; and how shamefully lax are Christians in the matter of giving of their substance for the maintenance of God's work. To this situation Malachi still speaks.[7]

REVIEW QUESTIONS

1. What is known about the man Malachi? What does his name mean literally?

2. When did Malachi prophesy? He was a contemporary of what other Bible author?

3. Who apparently was ruling Israel when Malachi wrote?

4. Name some of the sins of the Israelites that the book condemns.

5. What prominent feature appears eight times in the book?

6. Can you recall one outline of the book's message?

7. How does the book end? (4:4-6).

7. W. Graham Scroggie, *Know Your Bible* (London: Pickering & Inglis, 1940), 1:218.

Lesson 11
"Will a Man Rob God?"

A ll four chapters of Malachi are the subject of this last lesson of the study manual. You will probably want to divide the lesson into smaller study units because of the length of the Bible text. A suggested breakdown into three units is 1:1–2:9; 2:10–3:15; 3:16–4:6.

The apostle Paul was not excluding Malachi when he wrote of the Scriptures: "All Scripture is given by inspiration of God, and is profitable for doctrine, for reproof, for correction, for instruction in righteousness: that the man of God may be perfect, thoroughly furnished unto all good works" (2 Tim. 3:16-17). As you study the book of Malachi, continually look for these ways to apply it to your own life and to the lives of others.

I. PREPARATION FOR STUDY

Review Israel's history from its origin to the time of Malachi. What historical events and spiritual trends come to mind as you think of the following periods (listed chronologically)?

Patriarchs (Abraham, Isaac, Jacob, Joseph)
Bondage (in Egypt)
Exodus (escape from Egypt)
Judges
Kings
Captives
Restoration

What kind of a heritage did the Jews of Malachi's time have? Had they learned from their own history?

THE CONFRONTATIONS OF ISRAEL AND JEHOVAH

PROSECUTION	DEFENSE	REPLY AND VERDICT
Jehovah Charges	Israel Challenges	Jehovah Answers
1 1:2a	1:2b	1:2c-5
2 1:6a	1:6b	1:7a Ye offer polluted bread upon mine altar
3 1:7a Ye offer polluted bread upon mine altar	1:7b	1:7c-8
4 2:13	2:14a	2:14b-17
5 2:17a	2:17b	2:17c
6 3:7a	3:7b	3:8a Ye have robbed me
7 3:8a Ye have robbed me	3:8b	3:8c-12
8 3:13a	3:13b	3:14-15

II. ANALYSIS

Segments to be analyzed: 1:1–2:9; 2:10–3:15; 3:16–4:6
Paragraph divisions: at verses 1:1, 2, 6; 2:1, 10; 3:1, 7, 13, 16; 4:1, 4.
(Mark these in your Bible.)

A. General Analysis

This is a topical study of the Lord's charges against Israel for their sins, and of the defense that they put up to Him. You will have a good feel for the book's message when you have completed this study of the confrontations of Israel and Jehovah.
Record on the work sheet of Chart S the verses that represent prosecution, defense, and reply in each of the eight confrontations of Israel with the Lord. Note the following:
1. Israel's defense in each instance is introduced by the words "ye may" (e.g., 1:2). Each defense is a challenge of God's indictment.
2. At two points, the Lord's reply to Israel's challenge is the occasion for another challenge by Israel (see 1:7a; 3:8a on the chart).
3. Record in the right-hand column only a summary of the Lord's reply whenever the text is lengthy.
4. After you have completed recording this study, review the eight confrontations. What would you say were Israel's basic problems?

B. Paragraph Analysis

Now make a progressive analysis of the paragraphs as these appear on the survey Chart R. A few suggestions for study are given below.
1. *God's Love Rejected: 1:2-5*
How do the verses 1:3-5 illustrate God's love for the Jews? (Note: The Jews were descendants of Jacob; and the Edomites, enemies of Israel, were descendants of Esau.)
2. *Sins of the Priests: 1:6–2:9*
As you read the passage, note the different sins of the priests. What do verses 1:9, 11, 14 teach about God?

_____

_____

83

3. *Sins of the People: 2:10–3:15*

Read 2:10-17 in a modern paraphrase (e.g., *The Living Bible*). Then read the passage in the King James Version. What sins were the Jews guilty of?

_____

_____

Read 3:7-15. What sins are condemned here?

_____

_____

Read 3:1-6, then Mark 1:2-9. Who is the "messenger" of verses 2-8?

_____

Who came after that messenger had come (Mark 1:9)?

_____

_____

Is he the "messenger of the covenant" of Malachi 3:1? Is it possible that Christ's two comings are meant by these phrases: "he shall come"—first advent; "the day of his coming"—second advent? How would the prophecy of 3:1-6 be a message of hope for Malachi and his Jewish brethren?

_____

4. *Book of Remembrance: 3:16–4:3*

Observe the references to a coming day in each of the three paragraphs of this segment. When will that day be?

_____

_____

Who are the ones judged in each paragraph, and what are the outcomes?

_____

_____

Who do you think is the "Sun of righteousness" (4:2)?

_____

5. *Final Invitation and Warning: 4:4-6*

What is the command of verse 4?

_____

_____

How is the *heart* involved in this?

_____

_____

Read Nehemiah 1:5-7 to see how much importance Malachi's contemporary Nehemiah placed on the keeping of God's commandments.
What is the prophecy of verse 5? Compare this with 3:1*a*.

_____

(See *Notes* on Elijah the prophet.)
What ministry will Elijah perform, according to verse 6?

_____

What word closes the Old Testament? Of this, a footnote of the
Berkeley Version reads, "Fittingly the Old Testament ends with
the mention of a 'curse,' suggesting the need for the coming Messiah." G. Campbell Morgan comments:

> The last word is curse, but the last thought is not. The emphasis
> is on the word **Lest.** This suggests a way of escape from the
> curse. The curse is something to be prevented. It would fall if
> something were not done. That is the truth revealed in all the
> Law, the Prophets, the Writings.[1]

III. NOTES

1. *"I have loved you"* (1:2). The Hebrew tense of the verb
suggests continuity. G. Campbell Morgan comments, "It does not
look back only, but around and on, and I think may be rendered
for our more accurate apprehension, 'I have loved, I do love, I
will love you.'"[2]
2. *"I hated Esau"* (1:3). Read Romans 9:10-15. Paul here em-
phasizes that God's sovereign rejection of Esau was not an unrigh-
teous act. Burton L. Goddard says, "The 'hating' consisted of God's
perpetuating the line of the Chosen People through Jacob rather
than through Esau, and giving Esau a position subordinate to that
of his brother (cf. Gen 27:37-40)."[3]
3. *"Yet had he the residue of the spirit"* (2:15). Various interpretations of the first half of 2:15 have been made. Goddard suggests this paraphrase:

1. G. Campbell Morgan, *Searchlights from the Word* (Old Tappan, N.J.: Revell,
   1970), p. 299.
2. Morgan, *Voices of Twelve Hebrew Prophets*, p. 154.
3. Burton L. Goddard, "Malachi," in *The Wycliffe Bible Commentary*, p. 914.

And did not God make one pair to live together as one despite the fact that his control of the spirit of life could have been apportioned otherwise? And why did he make man and woman to be one flesh? It was to the end that his purposes for a godly seed, a covenant people of pure religion, might be realized.[4]

4. *"Elijah the prophet"* (4:5). John the Baptist was an *Elijah forerunner*, preparing the way for the Lord's first advent. (Read Matt. 17:12.) But there will also be an *Elijah forerunner* in connection with the Lord's second advent. (Cf. Mal. 4:5 with Matt. 17:11.)

IV. FOR THOUGHT AND DISCUSSION

1. What are your thoughts about God's sovereign election of Jacob to be an ancestor of the nation of Israel? (Be sure to read Rom. 9:10-15.)

2. Are the kinds of sins committed by the priests of Malachi's time being committed by Christian leaders of today? How can lay Christians deal with such a problem?

3. Does the *principle* of tithes and offerings (3:8) apply today? If so, how? For background of Old Testament origins of the tithe, read Leviticus 27:30-33; Numbers 18:20-32; Deuteronomy 14:22-29. Verses on offerings include Exodus 30:13; Leviticus 7:14; Numbers 15:19-21. A classic New Testament passage on Christian giving is 2 Corinthians 8-9.

4. The last verses of the Old Testament are about obeying God's commandments. What is the Christian's relationship to God's laws, such as the Ten Commandments? Are the commands of the New Testament essentially laws of God?

5. Does God keep "records" of a Christian's daily walk (see Mal. 3:16; 2 Cor. 5:9-10)?

V. FURTHER STUDY

With the help of outside sources, study Israel's history between the Old and New Testaments (400 B.C. to the birth of Christ).[5] This intertestamental period is sometimes called the "400 silent years." It was a time when God was preparing the world for the coming of His Son (cf. Gal. 4:4).[6]

4. *The Wycliffe Bible Commentary,* p. 916.
5. A description of this period, with many excellent maps is given by Jewish authors Yohanan Aharoni and Michael Avi-Yonah in the *Macmillan Bible Atlas* (New York: Macmillan, 1968), pp. 110-41.
6. See Irving L. Jensen, *Life of Christ* (Chicago: Moody, 1969), pp. 5-13, for a brief discussion of this.

A CONCLUDING THOUGHT

Four hundred years after Malachi wrote his book, a devout Jew, Simeon, was among those waiting for the Messiah to appear. One of the most beautiful pictures of the New Testament is that of the infant Jesus in the arms of Simeon at the Temple of Jerusalem, as the prophet blessed God, saying, "Lord, now lettest thou thy servant depart in peace, according to thy word: for mine eyes have seen thy salvation, which thou hast prepared before the face of all people; a light to lighten the Gentiles, and the glory of thy people Israel" (Luke 2:29-32). Are you among those who have begun to enjoy the fruits of that glorious salvation?

Bibliography

COMMENTARIES AND TOPICAL STUDIES

Baldwin, Joyce G. *Haggai, Zechariah, Malachi.* Downers Grove, Ill.: InterVarsity, 1972.

Davidson, F., ed. *The New Bible Commentary.* Grand Rapids: Eerdmans, 1953.

Earle, Ralph. *Meet the Minor Prophets.* Kansas City: Beacon Hill, n.d.

Feinberg, Charles L. *Malachi: Formal Worship.* New York: American Board of Missions to the Jews, 1951.

Gaebelein, Frank E. *Four Minor Prophets.* Chicago: Moody, 1970.

Kaiser, Walter. *Malachi: God's Unchanging Love.* Grand Rapids: Baker, 1984.

Lange, John Peter, ed. *Commentary on the Holy Scriptures:* Minor Prophets. Grand Rapids: Zondervan, n.d.

Pfeiffer, Charles F., and Harrison, Everett F., eds. *The Wycliffe Bible Commentary.* Chicago: Moody, 1962.

RESOURCES FOR FURTHER STUDY

Archer, Gleason L. *A Survey of Old Testament Introduction.* Chicago: Moody, 1964.

Baxter, J. Sidlow. *Explore the Book.* Grand Rapids: Zondervan, 1960.

Jensen, Irving L. *Jensen's Survey of the Old Testament.* Chicago: Moody, 1978.

———. *Minor Prophets of Israel.* Bible Self-Study Guide. Chicago: Moody, 1975.

———. *Minor Prophets of Judah.* Bible Self-Study Guide. Chicago: Moody, 1975.

New International Version Study Bible. Grand Rapids: Zondervan, 1985.

Payne, J. Barton. *The Encyclopedia of Biblical Prophecy.* New York: Harper, 1973.

Robinson, George L. "The Book of Zechariah." In *The International Standard Bible Encyclopedia,* vol. 5. Edited by James Orr. Grand Rapids: Eerdmans, 1952.

Ryrie Study Bible. Chicago: Moody, 1985.

Schultz, Samuel. *The Old Testament Speaks.* New York: Harper, 1960.

Strong, James. *The Exhaustive Concordance of the Bible.* New York: Abingdon, 1890.

Taylor, Kenneth N. *The Living Bible.* Wheaton, Ill.: Tyndale, 1971.

Tenney, Merrill C., ed. *The Zondervan Pictorial Bible Dictionary.* Grand Rapids: Zondervan, 1963.

Unger, Merrill F. *The New Unger's Bible Dictionary.* Chicago: Moody, 1988.